teletubbies
on the screen and behind the scenes

teletubbies
on the screen and behind the scenes

by denise noe

BearManor Media
2019

Teletubbies *On the Screen and Behind the Scenes*

© 2019 Denise Noe

All rights reserved.

No portion of this publication may be reproduced, stored, and/or copied electronically (except for academic use as a source), nor transmitted in any form or by any means without the prior written permission of the publisher and/or author.

Published in the United States of America by:

BearManor Media

4700 Millenia Blvd.
Suite 175 PMB 90497
Orlando, FL 32839

bearmanormedia.com

Printed in the United States.

Typesetting and layout by John Teehan

ISBN—978-1-62933-510-0

This book is dedicated to one of the long grown-up fans of Teletubbies, *my late, and deeply mourned, mother Betty Jo Dickerson (1930-2019).*

Table of Contents

An Enchanting Show Debuts… and *Continues* 1

The Creation of *Teletubbies* 11

Behind the Scenes of *Teletubbies* 25

Controversy: Talking 'Bout Baby Talk 37

Major Hit… Major Change 45

Photo Section 54

Controversy: Is Tinky Winky Gay? 63

Tubby Bye-Bye 73

2015 *Teletubbies* Say Eh-oh Again! 81

Thinking About All Things *Teletubbies* 97

Bibliography 107

Chapter 1

An Enchanting Show Debuts... and Continues

THE BRITISH BROADCASTING CORPORATION, popularly known by its initials BBC, is a world famous public service broadcaster of Great Britain. Its first broadcast Channel is BBC1 and its second is BBC2. Both stations air a varied range of programming, with BBC1 tending more toward mainstream, popular programs while BBC2 leans more toward sophisticated, highbrow types of shows.

On March 31, 1997, a new morning half-hour long children's television show entitled *Teletubbies* debuted on BBC2. The debut episode of *Teletubbies* was called "Ned's Bicycle."

As the episode begins, the screen fills with rolling green hills dotted with flowers and shrubs. A glowing sun, its rays pointing all around, rises over the horizon. The smiling face of a blue-eyed baby is inside that sun and a baby's delighted giggling and gurgling is heard. Light-hearted, tinkly music plays in the background as we see grass and flowers. We then see a structure built into the ground that is domelike and appears to have grass as part of its roof. Semi-circular openings on the sides of this structure appear to be its doors.

The friendly voice of an unseen adult female announces: "Over the hills and far away, Teletubbies come to play!"

From a hole atop the dome, a furry creature pops out, followed by three more. As they pop into view, a male voice enthusiastically announces, "One... two... three... four!" All four are in solidly colored cloth costumes, each sporting a large mask-like face with big eyes and ears, softly curving noses, and mouths that seem to be in permanent smiles. Each creature boasts an antenna protruding from the top of the head and a screen in the middle of his or her stomach.

The male voice, apparently that of the main narrator, exclaims, "Teletubbies!" As he does so, the word "Teletubbies" appears on the screen in letters that look as if they were formed out of balloons. "Voice Trumpets," silver-colored devices that look like metal periscopes, rise from the ground as the Teletubbies merrily dance around them. The man enthusiastically repeats, "Time for Teletubbies! Time for Teletubbies!"

Sounding very happy-go-lucky, the narrator tells the viewers the names of these odd but oddly inviting beings: Tinky Winky, the largest, is purple with a triangle antenna; Dipsy is green with a straight antenna that is like a dipstick; Laa-Laa is yellow with an antenna that curls before going straight; and Po, the smallest, is red with an antenna that has a round top resembling a soap-bubble tool.

The Tubbies get into a single file and march in a speeded-up manner reminiscent of the sort of sped-up gags for which British comedian Benny Hill was known and that are more generally used in film and TV comedy throughout the world.

Tinky Winky and Dipsy are on a hill together and playfully bump their tummies together. On another hill, Laa-Laa and Po do likewise. The four Tubbies get together, happily grasping each other, and saying all together in friendly childlike voices, "Big hug!"

When the four colorful characters are no longer on the screen, a Voice Trumpet rises up from the ground and a female voice asks, "Where have the Teletubbies gone?"

The giggling, gurgling Sun Baby appears again. Rabbits hop around the grassy area. The scene cuts to the inside of a building that appears technologically "futuristic" in architecture and decoration. There is a slide and each colorful Teletubby slides down that slide to get inside of what the audience by now figures to be the home of the Teletubbies.

The Tubbies gather around a large, silver-colored machine. They wave at the audience and say, "Eh-oh!"

The narrator declares: "It was time for Tubby Toast!" The Teletubbies excitedly echo, "Tubby Toast! Tubby Toast!" Tinky Winky, Dipsy, and Po gather around a table. Laa-Laa puts her arms in the air, and says, "Tubby Toast!" She then pushes a large button on the side of the machine. Pink buttons light up one after another. Slices of Tubby Toast file to the table at which the Teletubbies have gathered. Each Tubby Toast falls into a round plate in front of a seated Teletubby. Tubby Toast is round, light brown, and decorated by a simple smiley face. The Teletubbies excitedly munch on Tubby Toast.

The windmill that is outside begins slowly turning. "Unh-oh!" the Tubbies exclaim. They head out a door of the unusual home. The windmill is spinning faster and giving off pink sparkles. The four characters gather on the grass. They hug, lie on the ground and merrily swing limbs as their antennas and belly screens glow. Then they stand up again. Their antennas and tummies light up as they are now in a row and proudly say their names: "Tinky Winky!" "Dipsy!" "Laa-Laa!" "Po!"

The antennas and tummies dim. Then the antenna and tummy of Tinky Winky light up and the other three Tubbies gather 'round Tinky Winky. The show goes from Teletubbyland to a short film that is playing on the screen that is a part of this Teletubby's belly.

In that brief film, a helmeted small child rides energetically around an urban street on a scooter. He is soon inside a modern house playing with toys and making baby talk. Dad is there working on a bicycle. At one point, the child waves a little flag around. Dad and child look at the bicycle.

The scene cuts back to Teletubbyland. The Teletubbies look at Tinky Winky's tummy TV set and playfully demand, "Again! Again!" The short film about "Ned's Bicycle" is shown a second time.

After that second showing, the screen again fills with Teletubbyland. A narrator states, "One day in Teletubbyland, something appeared." A flag appears. Po wanders by, pulls the flag up, and waves it around. Tinky Winky wanders by, cheerfully muttering, "Pinkle winkle, Tinky Winky, pinkle winkle, Tinky Winky." He sees Po waving the flag. Tinky Winky asks, "Wha that?" "Flag!" Po happily exclaims.

Po holds the flag and both she and Tinky Winky march over the hills and between trees. They encounter Dipsy and Laa-Laa. Po and Tinky Winky march past the other two Teletubbies and to the front of the Teletubby House. Dipsy and Laa-Laa catch up with the other two. All four of them gather together and say, "Big hug!" and the group hugs.

The Teletubbies, together with the "real" TV audience, then watch as an animated show appears in Teletubbyland. In this "magical show," animatronic animals march in pairs. Tigers, penguins, snakes, elephants, flamingos, butterflies, turtles, giraffes, and frogs alternately walk, slither, hop, and crawl by, all two-by-two.

After this segment, a Voice Trumpet pops up and announces, "Time for Tubby bye-bye!" Each of the Teletubbies waves at the audience and disappears from view. Then each of them pops up again and they all say, "No!" in a manner similar to that of children who do not want to go to bed at bedtime.

But the Voice Trumpet is firm and says, "Bye-bye" to each Tubby who in turn say goodbye and wave at the audience before appearing to disappear into a hole

A female voice says, "The sun is setting in the sky. Teletubbies say good-bye." Each of the Teletubbies approaches the top of the Domed Home and says and waves goodbye again before jumping into the hole. After Po does this, she pops up from the hole one last time for a final "Bye-bye." The Sun Baby sets and the credits roll and the first episode of *Teletubbies* is indeed over.

The episodes following this auspicious debut of cuteness would be similar in major respects, possessing the same setting, characters, and basic format.

"Eh-Oh" and Big Hugs

Teletubbies was a show with much deliberate repetition. Many of its scenes were identical in all episodes. Each *Teletubbies* episode would start as the initial one did, with the same shot of beautiful rolling green hills and the happy, giggling Sun Baby rising over the landscape. A voice would cheerfully announce, "Over the hills and far away, Teletubbies come to play." After that announcement, so strongly evocative of fairy tales and nursery rhymes, Tinky Winky, Dipsy, Laa-Laa, and Po would pop up from the top of their domed home. They would say "Hello!" pronounced as a baby-like "Eh-Oh!" This would be followed by saying "Big hug!" and happily hugging. The characters would next disappear from view and a Voice Trumpet would ask, "Where have the Teletubbies gone?"

The Teletubbies would engage in a variety of activities or adventures. In each episode, one Teletubby tummy screen would show a short film, typically one prominently featuring human children. After the short was shown, the Teletubbies would usually all say, "Again! Again!" and it would be shown a second time. Episodes frequently featured a "magical scene" similar to the one showing animatronic animals marching in pairs that was in the debut episode.

Each episode also had the same ending. The announcement would be made, "Time for Tubby bye-bye!" Each Tubby would wave at the audience and then disappear from view. The Tubbies would then pop up and say, "No." The firm authoritative Voice Trumpet would say, "Bye-bye to each colorful character who would disappear from view for good, after which the credits rolled.

As the episodes continued, the audience learned that each Teletubby had his or her own special cherished item. Tiny Winky possessed a magic handbag, Laa-Laa had a big round ball, Dipsy had a tall black-and-white speckled hat, and Po had a scooter on which she loved riding. The show's creators wanted these props to demonstrate concepts of special interest to the very young. The handbag expressed volume, the ball was there because babies and toddlers tend to be intrigued by spheres, the hat was good for role-playing, and the scooter helped the show demonstrate direction and movement.

Teletubbies viewers discovered that a fifth major character was not a Teletubby but a singularly inspired combination vacuum cleaner and pet named Noo-Noo. This bright blue and metallic creature is rectangular but rounded in shape and possesses big eyes and a vacuum nozzle on its front. Noo-Noo does not speak in words but makes slurping and sucking noises. Noo-Noo loves the Teletubbies and is very happy to do his major duty of keeping their home clean and tidy and is often seen industriously cleaning up their messes. However, sprightly Noo-Noo possesses a spirit of mischief and will sometimes cause havoc by vacuuming up the toys of the Teletubbies, which can lead to a Tubby or two or three or four chasing "naughty Noo-Noo" around the Teletubby home. As might be expected, Noo-Noo's bad behavior is inevitably set right before the end of the episode when Noo-Noo, who, after all, loves the Teletubbies, spurts out the forbidden item or items, restoring harmony to the world of the Teletubbies.

In the ensuing episodes of the show, the Teletubbies mirror the mental and emotional states of their target audience of small children because they take enormous excitement and joy in such activities as sitting down on a chair and getting up from it, jumping around, playing peek-a-boo, walking up and down hills, skipping, and going around bushes and trees. They happily bump tummies and run around. They also fall frequently but falling does not lead to hurt or harm as the Teletubbies like falling down and waving their limbs as they lie happily on the ground. Their trademark activity was probably Teletubbies saying "Big hug!" and then hugging each other.

Tubby Toast and Tubby Custard are the favorite food items of the Teletubbies. Tubby Toast pops out of the Tubby Toaster and plops down onto plates on the table around which the Teletubbies gather for their meals. Of course, while the fictional Teletubbies eagerly savor Tubby Toast, it is not something humans would relish as the props used as Tubby Toast were in fact made of foam.

Some *Teletubbies* episodes were structured around malfunctions of the Tubby Toaster. For example, there was an episode in which the Tubby Toaster went wild with making its product and Tubby Toast flies throughout the Teletubby home and even manages to fly outside it. Another oddity is seen in this episode because there is a Tubby Toast with a frowning face that contrasts with the usual smiley face. There are two episodes in which the Tubby Toaster makes so much Tubby Toast that big towers of Tubby Toast are created. In still another episode, the Tubby Toaster creates a gigantic single piece of Tubby Toast. In yet another episode, the Tubby Toaster makes too much Tubby Toast and leaves a Tubby Toast pattern on the table of the Teletubbies. There is an episode in which Tubby Toast comes out bouncy and bounces throughout the house. There is also an episode in which Tinky Winky makes a surfeit of Tubby Toast which he is somehow able to get into his bag, but later, when he opens the bag, pieces of Tubby Toast burst out and Teletubbyland is flooded with Tubby Toast.

Tubby Custard has mashed potatoes as a major ingredient but, since it is mixed with yellow and red acrylic paint, is another food item that would hardly be palatable to humans. The Tubby Custard is made by the Tubby Custard Machine, a device boasting a red button that causes the tap to squirt out Tubby Custard and a black and gray lever that lowers and raises the Tubby Custard Tap. There is also a big silver lever that controls the doors of the Tubby Custard Machine and puts a bowl onto a conveyor belt. There is a green switch that turns the Tubby Custard Machine on and causes pink lights to flash. There is also a pink button in the middle of the Tubby Custard machine. The process of making Tubby Custard can be quite messy and the Tubbies often wear bibs when creating or eating it.

In one episode, Tinky Winky finds that Tubby Custard has been spilled. "Who 'pilled the Tubby Custard?" he asks, leaving the "s" off "spilled" as a toddler might. He follows the pink tracks and comes across Dipsy. He asks if Dipsy "'pilled" the Tubby Custard and Dipsy answers, "No." There are still big pink splotches on the ground so Tinky Winky and Dipsy follow them together. They find Laa-Laa playing in a tutu. She says she did not "'pill" the Tubby Custard either. The three then walk to the Tubby Home and find Po fast asleep—the tell-tale pink splotches covering her feet! The other three realize: "Po 'pilled the Tubby Custard!"

There is an episode in which Dipsy accidentally spills Tubby Custard over his seat and—understandably—does not want to sit in it. In another episode, Po spills Tubby Custard on the floor and Tinky Winky slips on it. There is also an episode in which the Tubby Custard Machine goes hog wild in producing and the Teletubby home is flooded with Tubby Custard!

Po eats too much of the delicious Tubby Custard and gets a tummy ache from it in one episode. Children often eat too much of a favorite food so they were certainly apt to see their own experience reflected in Po's overeating. Po's stomach pains are aggravated by the hiccups! As people learn early, very early, bad often follows bad.

Storylines in this series often revolved around making messes, something that mirrored the real lives of its preschool audience. Any small child can, of course, strongly identify with the Teletubbies when they get into messes because making messes, along with cleaning them up—whether successfully or not-so-successfully—is inevitably a major part of childhood.

In many episodes, the Teletubbies slide down the slide to get into the Tubbytronic Superdome that is their "home-sweet-home." There are also instances in which they magically slide *up*! The Teletubbies merrily make music, learn songs, and go on walks and marches. In some episodes, the Teletubbies lose toys and look for them. There are episodes in which the Teletubbies fly kites, play catch, and wash items with Tubby Sponges. Po goes slow and very fast on her scooter, excitedly exclaiming, "Wheee! Wheee!" as she scoots in and out of the Teletubby Home and then up and down the hills of Teletubbyland. There were episodes that were explicitly educational in that they focused on a number like 5 or 3 or 9 or a specific color like pink or green.

The featured short "tummy" films were quite varied—but all of them related well to the intended audience of very young children. There were films focusing on pigs, lambs, chickens, kids painting with their hands and feet, children talking about the number 1 and taking turns standing on one leg, and kids tap dancing. There were episodes in which a tummy screen showed films of the jazz band King Pleasure and the Biscuit Boys performing a jazz version of such classic nursery rhymes as "Grand Old Duke of York," "See Saw Marjorie Daw," and "Humpty Dumpty" before an audience of enthusiastic children. In more than one episode, actress Tamzin Griffin plays "Funny Lady," putting on a show with a sock puppet in front of a group of youngsters.

The "magical scenes" were also both varied and enchanting. In some, a magical box sails through the air and lands on grass in front of the Teletubbies. The box opens to reveal such animatronic wonders as a merry-go-round and a dancing teddy bear. The teddy bear cheerfully tap danced. There were magical scenes in which a tree would appear and disappear with its leaves changing colors. There were other magical scenes featuring ships that appear and sail before disappearing and magical rainclouds and flowers. The parading animals in the debut episode appeared in subsequent episodes.

A very special and unique television show, *Teletubbies* was the result of the combined imaginative vision of two very special and highly creative individuals.

Chapter 2

The Creation of *Teletubbies*

THE CO-CREATORS OF *TELETUBBIES* were Anne Wood and Andrew Davenport, both of whom had much experience with small children and a strong interest in promoting education and entertainment for the very young.

Wood was born to working-class parents in Spennymoor, County Durham, England. Her father was a road worker who was active in his trade union. An article in *The Guardian* quotes her as saying, "I had a father who would always tell me to think for myself. I was brought up in that sort of dissenting household." She showed academic promise from an early age. Her family encouraged her to pursue her intellectual interests and develop her talents into skills. As a young adult, she began a career as a secondary schoolteacher. In the 1960s, as both a teacher and mother of young children, she took an especially strong interest in teaching children to read and leading them to want to read. *The Guardian* reports, "Wood became passionately interested in what books children liked, why they read and—more importantly—why they didn't read."

Because of her strong interest in children's reading, Wood founded a magazine in 1965 called *Books for Your Children*—its purpose clearly stated in its title. The quarterly soon had a robust circulation and its success led book publishers and television businesses to ask Wood to consult with them on the content of material that was oriented to children. Eventually, this consulting work led to a job as a children's TV producer. She worked first for Tyne Tees Television, a television franchise for North East England as well as areas of North Yorkshire. Later, Yorkshire Television (now called ITV Yorkshire), a television service for the Yorkshire area, employed her to produce a children's show called *The Book Tower*, a television program that tried to interest its young audience in reading by having passages from both classic and modern books read aloud and scenes from books given brief dramatic presentations.

After TVAM, the United Kingdom's first commercial morning television franchise, was launched in early 1983, the new company asked Wood to develop a children's department and Wood did so. One of her first, and most outstanding creations, was the television show *Roland Rat: The Series*. The flamboyant puppet character of Roland Rat, known for his pink Ford Anglia car, was a big hit with British youngsters. The Ragdoll website recounts, "This anarchical character, with mis-spelt captions and chaotic interviews, satirizing the serious content of the breakfast show, proved hugely popular with children and their parents and began to reverse the declining ratings for the station." Wood has said she is "very proud" of creating Roland Rat. At the same time that Wood worked as producer for the series about the raucously madcap rodent, she helped create a magazine-style kiddie show called *Rub-a-Dub-Tub*.

Management changes at TVAM led to budgetary constraints which, in turn, led to drastic changes in children's programming. Wood parted ways with TVAM.

In 1984, Wood started her own production company. The name she bestowed upon that business reflected what was going on in her personal life. Wood's daughter, Katherine Wood, was a child at the time and cherished a rag doll she had named Jemima. Little Katherine Wood adored taking Jemima on adventures of the imagination. She also loved playing with the toy so much that a grandmother often put mending skills to good use to prevent Jemima from quite literally coming apart at the seams.

Wood decided to name her business after her child's treasured toy. Thus, the company that would do so much for children's television programming was christened Ragdoll.

The first program of the new company was *Pob*. The Ragdoll website describes the endearingly oddball title character as "a sort of 'goblin baby' who lived in the TV and interrupted normal transmission. Pob knocked on the back of the screen and then introduced himself by writing his name on the screen." Like Roland Rat, Pob was a puppet. In the show, Pob often interacted with grown-up guests.

Other kiddie programs produced in the 1980s by Wood's company included *The Magic Mirror*, which showed animated fairy tales, and *Boom!*, a show featuring special needs children.

The 1990s saw Ragdoll gracing British TV screens with more shows that helped brighten the lives of the country's youngsters. One of the most popular was *Rosie and Jim*. The title characters were puppets who explored Great Britain from their beloved boat called—what else?—*The Ragdoll*.

Another Ragdoll production from the same decade was *Brum*, in which an automobile possesses advanced intelligence so great that it not only drives itself but battles wicked doings in the city of Birmingham, England. The car's name is short for Brummagem, a colloquial term for the city. Yet another children's television show created by Ragdoll was *TotsTV* in which three rag doll puppet friends, Tilly, Tom, and Tiny, share a country cottage as well as participate in a series of adventures.

Of course, the most famous Ragdoll show is the one that is the subject of this book—*Teletubbies*.

Andrew Davenport, the man who would someday be admiringly called "the J. K. Rowling of the under fives" was born in Folkestone, Kent, England. He attended the Hayes School and then went to University College London and the National Hospitals College of Speech Sciences (NHCSS). He earned a degree in speech science. During his time attending University College London, he served as the school's Drama Society President.

After Davenport graduated, he and a performing partner, Kate France, formed their own theater company. This company performed before the Institute of Contemporary Arts and the Serpentine Gallery in London, England as well as the Richard Demarco Gallery in Edinburgh, Scotland, the *Théatre de la Bastille* in Paris, France and the Yermolova Theatre in Moscow, Russia.

In 1993 Davenport went to work for Ragdoll, creating and puppeteering the character of Tiny, the youngest and smallest of the major characters, in *Tots TV*. Davenport eventually began writing scripts for *Tots TV*. Wood was impressed by Davenport's work and liked working closely with him. The two of them, as well as others working for Ragdoll, were always on the alert for ideas that might lead to good children's programming.

One time, the two of them happened to be aboard an airplane when the film screen displayed a *Power Rangers* show. Viewing the superheroes of that American entertainment "action" franchise led Wood to muse on the possibility of taking an opposing approach. Wood recalled, "The *Power Rangers* were kicking each other and I told Andy that I would like to create characters who were the opposite of *Power Rangers* and who would not want to kick each other but to give each other a big hug and love each other." Thus, the seed for a peaceful, affectionate kind of anti-*Power Ranger* group of characters was planted.

Concerns that Wood harbored about very young children and how they responded to media nourished that seed. Ragdoll Productions launched studies of children's reactions to television shows such as *Tots TV* and *Rosie and Jim*. The company put considerable time, effort, and resources into examining how different sorts of programs were viewed by children. Youngsters were recruited for focus groups at Ragdoll Productions where they were shown various videos. The children were observed in how they responded to the videos and interviewed about their thoughts on them. Ragdoll also set up environments in which kids could play so that their "natural" actions could be taped and examined in the belief that good children's programming must relate to the sorts of things in which children are apt to be interested. "We became aware that there were still children, very young children, who could get a lot more from television and we hadn't quite reached far enough down to them," Wood observed. Wood believed a television show specifically crafted to the cognitive and emotional level of babies and toddlers—children between the ages of one and four and perhaps even including babies who had not yet celebrated their first birthdays—would fill a void and perform a public service. To that end, researchers at Ragdoll Productions studied the special qualities of the youngest children. "We began to discuss and think about how very young children perceive the world, which is different than the rest of us," Wood comments.

AN ASTRONAUT IRONY

Davenport had long been enthralled by space exploration and this interest led him to some very creative musings. "I was fascinated by the moon landings," he says. "It struck me as funny that, at this pinnacle of human achievement, the figures that emerged in bulky spacesuits from landing capsules are like toddlers, with oversized heads and foreshortened legs—and they respond to the excitement of their new world by bouncing about."

On an occasion when the collaborators were discussing possible characters for a kids' program, Davenport showed Wood drawings he had made of "space"-type characters who cheerfully hug each other and fall down without any pain or injury. He drew the space creatures with "baby proportions" and as "quite tubby" because they reminded him of babies and toddlers who tend to be on the "tubby" side. He also told Wood of his concept that the space beings lived in a magical wooded area in someone's garden. In an interview appearing in *Big Hug: The Story of the Teletubbies*, a 1998 BBC documentary, Wood said she found the drawings "hilarious."

Davenport, Wood, and Ragdoll as an organization were all destined for a big break when the BBC sought proposals for crafting a new show that would attract an audience of extremely young children. "The BBC wanted a new show for pre-schoolers and asked our company, Ragdoll, to pitch," Wood recalled. "We were interested in how children were reacting to the increasingly technological environment of the late 1990s."

Anna Home was BBC Head of Children's Programs from 1986 to 1997. "Commissioning any pre-school program is quite risky," she avers in *Big Hug*. "Because the great British public always thinks that what went before was better. There's always a kind of great nostalgia attached to pre-school programming."

Trying to decide what Ragdoll would pitch to the BBC, Davenport and Wood talked about the space being characters Wood had found so "hilarious" and tried to see how they could craft them into something that the BBC would want to put before small children.

The two talked about creating a little world for these tubby, loving, happily clumsy characters. They decided the show ought to have more than just two characters. Davenport projected a show about "characters based on spacemen, with limited language just like the emergent speech of young children." He also imagined the characters not as puppets or animatronic characters but as being played by human beings in big "tubby" costumes.

REELING IN THE REAL KIDS

The BBC wanted actual children featured in the series it commissioned. Davenport saw an immediate problem with real children interacting with the Teletubby characters. If they were played by adults in costume, they would be so large that children might be terrified of them. He commented, "Tinky Winky was 8 feet, 6 inches tall so the Teletubbies would have seemed like monsters to kids."

How could the world of real children be brought into the Teletubby world? Wood and Davenport discussed having the Teletubbies have their own big TV screen on which they watched the real kids. However, Wood noted that such a solution did not "organically" fit into the characters' world as it was envisioned. Equally important, the idea of the characters just watching their own TV was simply plain "boring." They wanted a solution with the sort of pizzazz that would capture the imaginations of a very young audience.

"Let's put TV screens on their tummies," Davenport suggested in a moment of inspiration.

"Then they'll have to have aerials on their heads!" Wood exclaimed.

Davenport recalls that he decided to put the TV screens in the particular part of the anatomy that he did, at least in part, because "for small children, your tummy is something you stick out and are proud of."

Additionally, Davenport wryly remarks, "I was entertained by the idea that the Teletubbies watch children on their screens with the same fascination that children watch Teletubbies on theirs."

Whether or not Davenport and/or Wood thought of it, having screens on the Teletubby bellies inevitably lent an aura of "mothering" to the characters (male or female). The motherliness conveyed by the tummy screens had to enhance the appeal of the characters to small children because it meant they automatically associated the Teletubbies with gentleness, nurturance, caring, and love.

For the projected show, Davenport also took inspiration from the humor of the famous English comedian Benny Hill who, as Davenport observes, often used "speeded-up film of people for his gags." Davenport believed children would enjoy watching the Teletubbies march or walk in the sort of sped-up way that is good for laughs.

Hoping to impress the BBC with their concept, Wood and Davenport created what Wood describes as "a picture book of technological babies" that they took to the BBC. When they got to the assembly at which competing ideas were to be pitched, Wood recalled that she and Davenport "were unnerved to find that the 11 other companies bidding had brought lots of fancy equipment and technical displays."

Anna Home, head of BBC Children's Television at the time, remembers, "Some people performed with puppets and some people performed themselves."

What chance did Davenport and Wood's simple little book of pictures have? It turned out to be a better one than its initially disheartened creators feared. "I think everyone there who saw the drawings [from Wood and Davenport] thought we had something very different, very new, and very appropriate for the age range," Home astutely observed. The age range for the new show, as previously noted, was one-year-old to four-year-old or perhaps five-year-old children.

Odd though it may sound, Wood actually harbored fears about *winning* the BBC commission. "I wasn't sure I wanted the commission," she admits. "The 100 episodes required would have launched our comfortably small-scale company into new territory."

Ragdoll won. Wood, Davenport, and others at the company eagerly and conscientiously sought to show the BBC that its confidence in Ragdoll Productions was justified.

Wood has commented that the first item on the agenda after the initial victory was finding a suitable place to film the new show. Previous Ragdoll programs had been shot outdoors but the concept for *Teletubbies* required a very special outdoor setting. According to Wood, there was difficulty finding "anywhere with a suitable bowl-like dip."

However, a Warwickshire farmer named Rosemary Harding—upon whose land the 1990s Ragdoll series *Tots TV* had been filmed—agreed to rent a field for the new show. The Warwickshire field was located not too far from the Stratford-upon-Avon headquarters of Ragdoll Productions. Ragdoll dug the needed hole on its own.

Another obstacle appeared to block the show. People who lived in the area feared the filming of the new show would lead to unwanted attention and loss of privacy. Wood recalls "the locals started protesting about us. I had to make my case to the planning authorities, wondering how, if they refused me, I'd explain to the BBC that I'd spent 150,000 pounds digging a hole and might have to spend another 150,000 pounds filling it in. I assured them it was a low-key children's program and no one would be aware of the filming." This prediction may have been sincerely made but no one can see the future and it would prove spectacularly wrong.

The Teletubby costumes posed many challenges—but veteran costume designer Niki Lyons was up to meeting them. In an interview with this author, Lyons revealed that Anne Wood believed "the original drawings looked a bit scary and lumpy." Lyons told this author that since she "was not [Wood's] employee but merely a rather poorly paid freelancer" she "kept the heavy head pattern" even as she "redesigned and made the Teletubbies in my largish house in London." Lyons cheerfully noted that Wood was so pleased by the costumes that the grateful Wood "sent a bunch of flowers with a compliments slip at the end of the project."

The Voice Trumpets were created, in part, because Davenport had done research that indicated that extremely young children, especially babies, have difficulty watching and listening at the same time. The Voice Trumpets alerted the child viewers that they should *listen*.

WHO WILL PLAY THE TELETUBBIES?

Casting a show is always critical to its success or failure. The actors and actresses must not only be good performers but must "fit" their roles and possess the appropriate onscreen chemistry with each other. A program like *Teletubbies* faces special challenges since the performers are playing fantasy characters and must tailor their acting style to small children. "We had to audition hundreds of people to find actors who understood that they were not trying to be children but trying to appeal to them," Wood remembers. It was also vital that the actors and actresses not play over the heads of their very young audience. "The successful applicants had to develop their character's unique style of speech by recalling how they spoke as children," Wood notes.

The first performer cast was British comedian and actor John Simmit. Before he portrayed green Teletubby Dipsy, Simmit had played on a BBC show that aired in the early 1990s entitled *The Real McCoys*. Alex Nelson notes in an article for *News* that *The Real McCoys* "served as a launching pad for many black comedians." However, Simmit did not see a strong link between his performances on *The Real McCoys* and his casting as Dipsy. "If you see my set on it, you're unlikely to think, 'Hmmm, he's a possible candidate for a furry children's icon,'" Simmit sardonically remarked.

Simmit wanted a part on *Teletubbies* and was not above telling a fib to get it. At his audition, he was asked if he could sing. "I can't—but said, 'yes,'" he sheepishly admits.

Nelson asserts that *The Real McCoys* and *Teletubbies* had an important thing in common since "both ventures celebrated diversity and inclusion." Simmit says, "It was woven into Ragdoll Production's ethos and it showed in everything they produced. They trusted us in actually building the Tubbies' characteristics around our quirks." Thus, "Dipsy was created as a furry, funky Jamaican toddler. The tune he regularly hums as he walks along is my take on a classic reggae rhythm track from the legendary Jamaican Studio 1 label." Another interesting aspect to Dipsy that related to the performer playing him was that Dipsy's face was notably darker than that of the other Teletubbies.

British-Chinese actress and presenter Pui Fan Lee was cast as smallest of Teletubbies, the red Po with the circle antennae. Fluent in both English and Cantonese, the talented Lee was still in her teens when she started acting professionally, appearing in Central

TV's Junior Television Workshop and in such television programs as *Dramarama*, *Hardwicke House*, and *The Worst Witch*. She also played in the Julia Roberts motion picture *Mary Reilly*. Just as Simmitt bestowed a bit of the funky Jamaican on Dipsy, Lee gave part of her own background to Po. For example, Po would say "Faster, faster" as the Cantonese "Fi-dit, fi-dit," and, instead of saying "One, two, three," she would say those numbers as the Cantonese "Yat, yah, sáam." Wood was quoted in *The Guardian* commenting that Lee "struggled to find her Teletubby voice" in English so the show's makers decided Po should make use of the Chinese language that was Lee's "mother tongue."

Although Teletubbies were *Teletubbies*, not human beings, the program's makers said there was a sense in which Dipsy was intended to represent black people and Po was meant to represent Chinese people. Diversity and inclusion were indeed basic to the ethos of the show.

English actress, director, and choreographer Nikky Smedley was cast in the part of the curly-antennaed and yellow Laa-Laa. Interviewed by the writer of this book, she recalled how she got the part: "I answered an ad that said something like 'artist with stamina wanted for new children's TV show.' And then it said, 'People with interesting backgrounds and experience particularly wanted.' I thought, 'that's me' and auditioned."

Right from the start, Smedley strongly believed in the project. In an interview with a journalist from *The Telegraph*, she said, "When the show was explained to me, I thought it was a work of genius."

Comedian, actor, and writer Dave Thompson was cast as Tinky Winky, he of the purple suit and triangle antennae, in large part because of work he had done on another television program. "I played several characters in Harry Hill's first TV series *Harry Hill's Fruit Fancies*," he told this author of this book. "One of the characters I played was an Egyptian mummy. The costume lady had to sew the bandages over my face and I couldn't come out of the costume again until she had cut the stitches over my face with a pair of scissors." He elaborated that people inquired as to whether or not he felt "claustrophobic" in that mummy outfit. He assured them that he "felt safe and secure in there."

Another individual who worked on *Harry Hill's Fruit Fancies* went to work on *Teletubbies*. "He remembered me in the mummy costume and asked me to audition for the part of Tinky Winky," Thompson told this writer. "I was one of 600 people who auditioned for the role and I got the part."

CASTING OTHER PARTS

Jessica Smith, the daughter of Bill and Anji Smith, was nine months old when she was filmed to become the Sun Baby of *Teletubbies*. Her parents were paid 250 pounds as well as a box of toys to take home for the infant.

For many years, the identity of the Sun Baby was unknown to the general public. In 2014, young Jessica started attending Canterbury Christ Church University. During her first week at the educational institution, there was an event in which students were asked to tell secrets about themselves that they did not believe others would be likely to guess. She revealed her identity as the Sun Baby.

Actor Tim Whitnall was cast as the authoritative but friendly and reassuringly gentle off-screen narrator. He would also sometimes provide a Voice Trumpet. Whitnall already had an impressive résumé at the time of his *Teletubbies* casting, having played Jake in the TV series *The All Electric Amusement Arcade* (1983). He also played in episodes of *Summer Season* (1985), *C.A.T.S. Eyes* (1986), the TV mini-series *Cold Lazarus* (1996) and performed voice work for the short *Famous Fred* (1996).

Sandra Dickinson's enchantingly breathy and girlish voice was ideally suited to appeal to little kids which made her a perfect Voice Trumpet. She was a very experienced actress who had played in such

TV series as *The Tomorrow People* (1975), *The Hitchhiker's Guide to the Galaxy* (1981), and *The Clairvoyant* (1984-1986). She had done previous voice work in *The World of Peter Rabbit and Friends* (1992), *We're Back! A Dinosaur's Story* (1993), and *Balto* (1995).

Along with Whitnall, actor John Schwab supplied a masculine take to the Voice Trumpets. He had done previous voice work on the English version of a 1984 motion picture entitled *Nausicaä of the Valley of the Wind*.

King Pleasure and the Biscuit Boys made occasional appearances in the short Teletubby "tummy screen" film segments in part because Anne Wood and her family saw them perform at the Royal Shakespeare Theatre in Stratford. "She enjoyed the night and got in touch with us about an idea called *Teletubbies*," Mark Skirving, whose stage name is King Pleasure, told the author of this book. "She asked if we would like to appear on the show singing our own jazzy versions of nursery rhymes." The show benefited enormously because the group was more than happy to regale a preschool audience with nursery rhymes set to jazz.

Chapter 3

Behind the Scenes of *Teletubbies*

DAVENPORT AUTHORED ALL 365 *Teletubbies* episodes from 1997 through 2001. When writing a *Teletubbies* script, he was usually in an on-set caravan. He recalls that he often "lived for weeks on end" in that caravan "because I had to adapt to the capabilities of the performers." For example, "At the start, they said they couldn't walk on grass because their costumes were too unwieldy." The show was shot at the special part of the Warwickshire farm reserved for that purpose. Since there was no studio, indoor shots of *Teletubbies* were always done inside the Teletubby domed home.

The program was not on the air long before Wood realized her assurance that the show would receive little public attention had been way off base. Media attention to *Teletubbies* was intense. "We had photographers crawling across fields and hovering from helicopters," Wood remembers. A security firm was hired to guard the program setting. Wood says, "We were so keen to keep the location a secret, we would blindfold visitors."

Since so much of the program was shot outdoors, the filming of the program was inevitably influenced by a factor beyond human control, namely weather. "The worst times were when it had been raining for days, and I'd have to set the action indoors because it was too wet to film outside," Davenport recalls.

In an interview with this author, camera operator Ian Nelson remarks, "We were at the mercy of the weather up there so there would often be a rush to cover as much kit as possible from the impending downpour and then sit it out under golf umbrellas until we could film again."

On one occasion, the area had a violent rainstorm that put much of the set underwater. "We all sheltered in the dome, but water began bubbling through, and the fire brigade had to pump us out," Davenport says. "Several of us had to spend that night in Teletubbyland because the fields were too flooded to cross."

Recalling that rainstorm, Nelson told this author, "The whole site flooded." He continued that he and other crew members "managed to improvise a 'snorkel' for our van and get out through a sudden 4-foot deep fjord that had formed on the exit road." He also stated, "The Teletubby Dome flooded and the floor warped so we had to leave site while it was dried out and repaired."

Nelson told this author about another time disaster struck the *Teletubbies* set: "A model helicopter used to tow a polystyrene balloon across the sky crashed into the Teletubby Dome. No one was near it, thankfully, but there was one very upset helicopter owner. Some Astro Turf repairs had to be made to the Dome."

There is no question *Teletubbies* is a very special show. Simmit recalls thinking "while filming an early sketch and looking out from the suit at the others that the show was very strange." He was uncertain as to how it would be received, at the time musing, "It could've been a big success or disappeared quickly."

Costumes and Comfort

The Teletubbies lived in a sweet and lovely fantasy world. Their easy life was a marked contrast to the special challenges faced by the performers who had to work for long hours in the bulky Teletubbies suits. "It got very hot in the costumes and the show was filmed during the summer," Dave Thompson recalls. "I didn't mind getting hot as I knew the show would entertain millions of children."

In an interview with this author, Nikky Smedley readily admits that she found the Laa-Laa costume "very uncomfortable." She elaborates, "It weighed about 4 1/2 stone [63 pounds]. It was very tall and very cumbersome." Nevertheless, she believes the goal of creating a quality show made the discomfort more than worth bearing. "Besides all the discomfort and hard work, you always thought about the child watching at home and put the discomfort out of your mind to bring that child joy," she asserts.

What did Smedley like about playing Laa-Laa? "I liked being part of a project in which I had such great belief," she replies. "I also liked it because I met Anne Wood and Andrew Davenport—people of integrity and skill. Of course, the whole group that worked on the show was made up of really marvelous people, about 45 people who were really focused on making children happy."

Acting in any show requires putting in many hours, and acting in *Teletubbies* meant doing so in a large and heavy costume. "Fatigue was the most challenging thing about acting in the program," Smedley avers. "We had to keep our energy levels up and our performances fresh."

Although the bulk and heaviness of the costumes inevitably made them challenging to wear, the thick padding inside the costumes meant that, in some ways, they were remarkably comfortable. In the filming of any show, performers must spend much time just waiting as lights are rigged, props are put into place and removed, and cameras find their desired angles. The *Teletubbies* performers sometimes slept deeply in their thickly padded Teletubby suits, with their Teletubby heads in place, as they waited for the set to be made ready.

An actor or actress could not see out of the suits unless the mouth of the face mask was open. Thus, when a Teletubby mouth was closed, the actor or actress was, in effect, blind. Each performer operated the opening and closing of the mouth with the right hand and the opening and closing of the eyes with the left hand. Inside their costumes, the actors worked on levers that Thompson calls "just like the brake handles from a push bike." Wires went from the hand mechanisms to the eyes and mouths of the Teletubbies.

Occasionally a wire would snap on the set, causing a Teletubby mouth to gape open or the eyes to roll upwards and stick in that position. Thompson remembers, "This always caused much laughter on the set as it looked like the character had died."

A technician, who had previously served in the Royal Air Force, was responsible for repairing the eye and mouth mechanisms. According to Thompson, "The mechanics of the planes he worked on were similar to the mechanics of the Teletubbies."

Getting into these enormous costumes was hardly a breeze and each performer had two dressers to help the actor/actress get into his or her Teletubby costume. For all the challenges, acting in this show offered wonderful rewards, not only financially but artistically and emotionally.

In an interview with the author of this book, Thompson relates that he found playing Tinky Winky very satisfying. "I loved playing Tinky Winky because the Teletubbies have a mental age of three," he discloses. "I was paid lots of money to stay in a country house hotel, and run around a field in beautiful countryside behaving like a three-year-old."

Before filming each episode, the *Teletubbies* actors and actresses first did a read-through and then a walk-through rehearsal. "At the beginning it was new to all of us so it took some getting used to but once we got into the swing of it, it was really simple," Thompson says.

Although the performers spoke their lines as they filmed, the actual soundtrack was, of necessity, over-dubbed post-production. "This is because there was too much ambient sound on-set to use the soundtrack recorded during filming," Thompson explains. Another reason what was recorded during filming could not be used in the showing of the program was that, when the Teletubby mouths were opened and closed, mechanisms in the jaw parts of the masks made noises.

A situation that would prove somewhat ominous was when Thompson stopped doing the verbal part of Tinky Winky during the first season. "At first they asked me to do a high voice and then they changed their minds just before we started filming," Thompson recalls. Actor Mark Heenehan was hired to be the voice of Tinky Winky.

When the series first started filming, instructions were given to the performers through a loud-hailer (which is called a bullhorn in the United States and Canada). This was soon exchanged for fitted ear pieces that went into the ears of the performers (not the oversized ears of the Teletubby masks) so instructions were sent electronically.

Shooting *Teletubbies* provided special challenges, according to camera operator Nelson. "Live action full-sized actors in costumes and often digital/model effects shots to be composited in later whereby we had to guess at the space required in frame for that all to work," Nelson relates.

As might be expected, making this series was not trouble-free. The Voice Trumpets emerged in their periscope fashion out of narrow but deep holes in the ground. When a Voice Trumpet was not in use, a cover similar to a manhole cover was placed over the Voice Trumpet hole. There was an occasion when someone forgot to cover a Voice Trumpet hole. Thompson reveals, "I was being filmed running along when my right foot went straight down the deep hole. I could have broken my leg but thanks to my training in martial arts, I had the awareness to stop putting weight on the leg that went down the hole. As a result, my leg wasn't injured."

Some stunts were especially demanding and required workers specifically trained in stunts like Tom Delmar, an experienced stunt coordinator who sometimes worked on *Teletubbies*. In an interview with this author, he recalls how he got his first *Teletubbies* gig. "I got the call whilst filming on a movie called *The Lost Son*," he discloses. His first work on *Teletubbies* was not his last. "I worked occasionally when silly jumps or bumps were needed," he remarks. In one episode, he donned the purple Tinky Winky suit to flamboyantly fall down a hill.

According to Delmar, Tinky Winky's favorite toy could present a special challenge in performing a stunt. "The biggest problem was the handbag getting in the way," Delmar states. He adds that there were "issues jumping down rabbit holes." As well as falling down a hill and jumping down a rabbit hole, Delmar-as-Tinky Winky also "fell off boxes."

That stunts would be both needed and challenging makes sense as *Teletubbies* was a program for small children who tend to respond well to boisterously physical comedy.

The cast and crew of *Teletubbies* were dedicated to making a good show for pre-schoolers and their belief in their mission helped make their jobs satisfying and their relationships with each other appropriately cooperative. When this writer asked Smedley how she got along with cast and crew, she answered, "Wonderfully. There were about 45 of us altogether in the English countryside so we all did a fantastic job of making it fun and we had a joyful atmosphere." Thompson told this author that cast and crew had few conflicts. "The crew were mostly young and very pleasant to get on with," he asserts.

For camera operator Ian Nelson, the setting and company both contributed to fond memories. "It was a beautiful location with some of the best crew I've worked with so I spent five lovely summers up there in my twenties," he told this writer.

WORKING WITH RABBITS, WORKING WITH KIDS

Rabbits eating grass and hopping around Teletubbyland were an enchanting part of the show. Since they had to visually fit into the environment, only unusually large rabbits would do. Thus, a special breed, the Flemish Giant, was enlisted for the series. "The only suitable [rabbits] we could find had been bred on the continent to be eaten," Wood comments. "We gave them perfect conditions, running free over the Teletubby grasslands, but their breeding had given them enlarged hearts and, almost weekly, the animal trainer would greet me in distress and tell me another had died." Many rabbits were used in filming an episode; several perished during the show's run. "At least they died happy," Wood observes.

Rabbits will be rabbits and their behavior was not always suitable for the *Teletubbies* audience of small children. The bunnies frequently mated which necessitated interrupting some takes and re-shooting others.

Actress Nikky Smedley told this author that she received amusement from the *Teletubbies* rabbits—and other rabbits as well while working on the series. "Sometimes some normal-sized rabbits would appear on the set," she recalls. "They would circle around our giant rabbits like our rabbits were gods. That made me laugh every time I saw it happen."

As previously noted, the show was not on long before media inundated the program's setting. Davenport felt it was important to maintain the illusions of the show's target audience of pre-school children and did not like the way some journalists appeared to want to shatter those illusions. "Photographers' main goal seemed to be to get pictures of the Teletubbies without their heads on," he observed. "So we had to build a tent in the corner of the field where they could remove them in secret. It felt like the press was trying to tell kids that Santa Claus didn't exist."

Kids will be kids and King Pleasure/Mark Skirving recalled an incident that was at once "challenging" and "enjoyable/funny." The band's jazz-swing version of the classic nursery rhyme "Hey Diddle Diddle" was being filmed when, he says, "One of the children who came running over to us kept grabbing the microphone from in front of the guitar amp and singing excitedly into it. The director would have to cut, explain to the lad that he mustn't do it and get everyone back into position for a re-take. This happened four times in a row before he eventually got the message and stuck to dancing."

Camera operator Ian Nelson worked on most *Teletubbies* episodes. The job on the series was an important milestone in his career. "It was my first long-term gig as a camera operator," he told this author. "The whole project was just so bizarre compared with any other job that it was just the best time and I doubt I'll ever top it." He fondly remembers a special perk: "Offsite, one of my favorite memories is trips up the Avon on our lighting director's narrow boat on which he lived while filming up there."

The "tummy film" of a *Teletubbies* episode entitled "Flamenco Guitar" featured Tito Heredia, an actor, guitarist, and guitar instructor. How was Heredia chosen to appear in the series? "Through an agency," he told the author of this book. In the short film, Heredia entertains children by playing his guitar. What did he strum on the guitar? "It was just spontaneous guitar work, moving with the children, then a sort of flamenco version of 'Pop Goes the Weasel,'" he said. He elaborated that what he liked most about making the film was "the reaction of the children to the music." What he found most challenging was "keeping the piece flamenco, interesting to the children, [and] without complexity."

"Delilah Packing" was the simple title of one *Teletubbies* episode in which the short film featured two sisters, Delilah and Cecilia, packing up their bags for a trip to "Mim's" [the children referred to a grandmother by her nickname "Mim"]. The featuring of these kids in *Teletubbies* came about in a sort of roundabout fashion. Their Dad, Peter Dumont, recalls meeting a young lady who was working on a project and asked if she could film the kids on her video camera for it. He continues that she seemed "especially enamored" of Delilah and Cecilia. "That was fine by me because I agreed with her judgment that my children were precocious and stars," he wryly remarked. "They still are." At a certain point, the woman who had filmed the sisters on her camera for her own project revealed that she was connected with Anne Wood and *Teletubbies*. The father of Delilah and Cecilia was quite happy that his daughters would have a chance to be on the children's show. "It was decided in advance to film an event that could be predicted but was by no means a regular occurrence," he revealed. The children often stayed overnight with their maternal grandmother to "give the parents" a night off, he continued. Thus, packing for that overnight stay became the subject of the Teletubby tummy film.

Cecilia Dumont told this writer she did not remember the day of the filming too clearly because of her young age but does recall, "I was quite quiet and in my own world and this shows in the footage. Delilah was more enthusiastic about being able to show off her packing system to the camera crew. This is where she was in her element as a child. We were very close though and she did always pack our bags for both of us."

Appearing on *Teletubbies* is fondly remembered by Cecilia. "It has become quite a funny thing to be able to say I was in the show, it's what I rely on in that awkward situation where someone asks you what your party trick is or to tell them something interesting about yourself," she told this author. "My friends seem to find it hilarious that I was on the *Teletubbies*, too, and always want to bring it up at gatherings. I personally think there should be a *Teletubbies* reunion show or something to do with the kids, like us, who were also in the show."

Jane Lambert and her daughter Olivia Lambert appeared in a 1997 *Teletubbies* episode entitled "I Want to Be a Vet" after Olivia's childhood career goal (as an adult, Olivia actually became a science teacher). The tummy film begins with the little girl's face being seen. The camera pulls back and we see the little girl is with her mother and the mother is holding a little cage. Viewers soon learn that a rabbit, mostly white with black markings, is being brought to a veterinarian for an examination. The little girl announces her desire to practice the same profession as the veterinarian examines the teeth of the bunny Olivia calls "Thumper." Interviewed by this author, Jane Lambert revealed that, once again, the size of a rabbit was a consideration in *Teletubbies*. "The rabbit in the film was not ours," she states. "Our rabbit was a miniature rabbit and was far too aggressive to appear in the film so we borrowed the very lovely, large rabbit from the school secretary" of Chater Infants School. Jane Lambert has fond memories of her work in the *Teletubbies* episode. "It was a lovely experience," she wrote to this author. "I still enjoy looking at the film (now on YouTube). Lots of our friends enjoyed watching it and funnily enough my sister-in-law even saw a (dubbed) Spanish version of the same episode when she was visiting relatives in Spain who were very impressed with our Spanish speaking!"

A physician for the Homo sapiens was featured in a short entitled "My Mum's A Doctor." The brief film focused on a little girl named Jenny Crook and her mother, Dr. Helen Gabathuler. The latter explained how she and her daughter got to appear on *Teletubbies* in an interview with the author of this book. "Through a hospital doctor friend whose GP (general practitioner) husband worked with my husband," Dr. Gabathuler related. "The former had a friend (through their children) who worked on the show, and had asked her if she knew any kids aged around five who had a mother who was a GP. Jenny was younger but very chatty so they thought of her and me." In the tummy film, Jenny and her Mum-the-doctor demonstrate an examination that a child would be likely to have when visiting a physician. Dr. Gabathuler is a GP and, in the short, used an auroscope to examine little Jenny's ears and throat and a stethoscope to listen to the child's breathing. "All program-watching small children would have had exactly some or all of those clinical examinations done whenever they had been taken to the GP with a non-specific or an infection illness," Dr. Gabathuler says. "Or seen siblings examined! I think the brief was just to demonstrate what we do." The doctor says she "wasn't really acting" to make the film. She enjoyed working for *Teletubbies* as it "was an interesting experience and something a bit different." The physician candidly admits she feels a certain "embarrassment" when she watched the film in which she appeared. Since the film had no major mistakes and she did not goof, why does she experience embarrassment?

"Have you never had that when watching yourself on video?" she wryly replies. Dr. Gabathuler was reminded of the experience when she "was contacted about five years later by a friend who was living in Australia to say she had just seen us on TV."

Chapter 4

Controversy: Talking 'Bout Baby Talk

CONTROVERSY DOGGED THE CHILDREN'S SHOW from the start. For one thing, fans of *Playdays*, the children's show that had previously aired on the slot taken by *Teletubbies*, were inevitably disappointed to see a show they treasured being replaced. Thus, the following letter appeared in the April 17, 1997 issue of BBC's weekly magazine *The Radio Times*:

> Mummy tells me that the new program *Teletubbies* is to help me to learn. I did like the purple one but that is my favorite colour, and I did learn how to say "uh-uh" which I never knew before, but I missed the stories and songs on *Playdays*.
>
> I don't know what to do for the rest of my day because on *Playdays* they showed me how to make something and then it took me all day to do it.
>
> I hope *Playdays* comes back to the mornings soon, but Mummy says it probably won't because too much money has been spent on *Teletubbies*.
>
> Katherine Caunter (aged 3)
> Seaford, Lincolnshire

Many people had concerns about the new show that went far beyond nostalgia for the program it replaced. Concerned parents wrote letters to *The Radio Times* complaining that the toddler-like speech of the Teletubbies would delay the ability of small children to learn correct language. After all, babies naturally make "baby talk" when learning and no one wants to *teach* baby talk. Other British media venues picked up on this concern and ran articles about the possibility that *Teletubbies* might be harmful to its very young audience.

Journalist Paul McCann in *The Independent* wrote, "This helped spark a debate about whether *Teletubbies* is dangerous nonsense or a highly sophisticated program that helps the language learning and thinking processes of the youngest television audience in history." McCann correctly observed that this spirited debate made the show "much more than 'only' a children's television program."

Stephen Byers, then spokesperson for Great Britain's Department of Education and Employment, blasted the "dumbing down" of British culture in answer to a question about *Teletubbies*. In *The Guardian*, Byers wrote, "Everyone knows the Teletubbies are 'slow, banal and ill-conceived,' not to say repetitive." Byers may have put "slow, banal and ill-conceived" in quotes because he believed these critical adjectives were commonly used to blast the program. *The Guardian* writer Judith Williamson wrote about "the widespread complaint that the Teletubbies are 'slow, silly, banal and incoherent,' that they are 'repetitive' and 'don't talk properly.'" Maggie Brown, another writer for *The Guardian*, observed, "Parents are angry that the Teletubbies don't talk properly; they say they are slow, silly, banal and incoherent, and that the program is aimed at children who are really too young to be watching TV at all."

Writing for *The Mirror*, Gill Swain noted that parents objected to the "goo-goo style" of *Teletubbies* as well as "the repetitive phrases the creatures use." Swain quoted Liz Duffy, a mother of three children, as complaining, "*Teletubbies* is boring and repetitive. The characters have ridiculous names and don't speak coherently. They say things like 'haro.' I have gone to some trouble to help my children speak clearly. The last thing I want to hear them say is 'haro.'"

Anne Wood acknowledges that the criticisms caused her discomfort: "Ever since *Teletubbies* first transmitted, I've felt that I've been on trial." Wood has also said, "I felt for a time I was being bullied."

Wood strongly maintains that the concern that *Teletubbies* "was not educational enough" was misguided. "There was an innocence, as well as a glorious silliness, to the series, which is why I never permitted it to become a pantomime because of the inevitable salacious jokes that would pollute it," Wood asserts. "We were trying to reflect children's experience back to them."

Andrew Davenport, who possesses a degree in speech sciences, also found the concerns misguided. "There is so much more to communication than just speech," he asserts. "But even so, it is a genuine language the Tubbies have. It has a proper grammatical structure and what they say is meaningful to the children."

Davenport was disdainful of the fear that the program he co-created would harm language acquisition in its pre-school audience. "The idea of it damaging their speech development is nonsense," he asserted. "Children learn to speak from the continuous real world and real people around them; a half-hour TV program is not going to affect that."

Under the heading "A Winner for the Tots," the May 8, 1997 *Radio Times* ran a letter to the editor by an adult observer who strongly supported *Teletubbies*.

> I write in response to a letter about BBC's *Teletubbies*. I'd like to say that as a qualified nursery nurse and registered child minder I am very aware of the important factors involved in early education.
>
> My three-year-old son James and the two four-year-old girls in my care have really enjoyed this series. They have been completely engrossed in the various activities in which the *Tektubbies* [sic] and children are involved. The children are also *Playdays*

fans, another educational, fun and stimulating programme. Variety is the spice of life.

Judith Challoner Edinburgh

To put matters in perspective, it should be noted that the *Teletubbies* narrator and the Voice Trumpets speak in an adult manner in sentences both clear and perfectly grammatical. What's more, the adults appearing in the short tummy films also speak in correct examples of the King's or Queen's English.

WHY SO MUCH "AGAIN! AGAIN!"?

Adults often expressed bewilderment at the repetition that was such a large part of this show. This repetition was perhaps most powerfully exemplified by the showing of the Teletubby "tummy short film," followed by the Teletubbies shouting "Again! Again!" followed by a second showing of the same short film. Davenport asserts that repetition is something children like and something that helps them. "I noticed children watching *Tots TV* who would fix on one concept and come back to it over and over again," he states. "It is because there is such a mass of stimulus to understand when they are young that repetition keeps things simple and familiar."

The "magical" scenes in the show also sparked criticism—which Davenport found unwarranted. One scene that some people believed was done poorly was the marching two-by-two of animals that occurred in the debut episode as well as some following episodes. "People asked why didn't we name the animals as they went past which is to completely misunderstand what we're doing," he comments. "The sequence was about rhythm which is essential for children's language learning, turn-taking and even simple mathematics later in life."

This chapter began with a letter from a child who was disappointed to see a show that she loved, *Playdays*, replaced by another show. Many grown-ups were also disappointed with this change and Wood's fear that at least some of the British public would be against the new show out of "nostalgia" for an old show was vindicated when, as Anne H. White reported in an essay on *Teletubbies*, *Radio Times* ran letters from disgruntled adult viewers "complaining about the decision to replace *Playdays*," widely considered a more "traditional" children's show, with *Teletubbies*. Indeed, one viewer blasted the BBC for "cultural vandalism" by replacing *Playdays*, a television series which the person called "a defining experience in the development of a whole generation." Of course, as White noted in her article, today many adults who watched *Teletubbies* as children regard *Teletubbies* as such a "defining experience."

As White also observed, *Teletubbies* got caught in "an on-going ideological struggle relating to educational standards in the UK, a war between the 'trendies' and the 'traditionalists.'" The traditionalists accuse the trendies of dumbing down children's educational programs.

On August 24, 1997, BBC Children's Television executive Anna Home told the attendees at the Edinburgh International Television Festival that children were not being harmed by the toddler-like talk of the Teletubbies. She drew an analogy with another kiddie program and observed, "The children who grew up watching *The Clangers* didn't grow up into a generation of whistlers." Or at least, it might be added, they certainly did not replace normal language with whistling!

The controversy continued as *Teletubbies* entered its second season and was seen in many countries outside the United Kingdom. At the 1998 World Summit on Television for Children, a prominent speaker faulted *Teletubbies*. Ada Haug, head of pre-school programming for the government owned radio and television broadcasting company of Norway, the NRK, made the by now familiar accusation that *Teletubbies* constituted a "dumbing down" of children's shows. Rob Brown, writing for the *Independent*, reported "She also criticized the constant repetition, the poor plots and the fact that the series had no sense of place."

However, Alice Cahn, head of children's programming for America's Public Broadcasting Service (PBS), would have none of that. "To suggest that *Teletubbies* signals a dumbing down is ludicrous," she declared. "It's the most old-fashioned but new-fangled program for young children I've ever seen."

CHILDREN'S RIGHT TO JUST PLAIN FUN

As the controversy heightened and went global, Anne Wood remarked, "I know people would like to make a wax image of me and stick pins in it. But children have a right to enjoy themselves."

Radio Times ran an "Editor's Letter" on June 5, 1997 about the show. "*Radio Times* readers in *Teletubbies* tumult!" that Editor's Letter began. "Your reaction to the BBC2 pre-school series that's ousted *Playdays* from its morning slot has made headlines. Which just goes to prove what you and I already knew: the liveliest debate to be found about television and radio is on these pages every week." The editorial went on to note the spirited and often emotional back and forth between supporters and detractors of the kids' series: "Our correspondents popped up in the newspapers and on television to question the educational value of creatures who talk like babies and look like aliens." The editorial wryly elaborated that "if it's any consolation" to the possibly offended "Tinky Winky, Dipsy, Laa-Laa and Po," the *Radio Times* "mailbag over the first two months of the series shows 50 per cent in favor of the Tubbies."

A couple of months later, on August 21, 1997, *Radio Times* published yet another letter about the controversial TV show for the little ones. That letter, by Louise Tinniswood Birtley, said its writer had "heard numerous complaints" regarding the series and "wondered what all the fuss was about." She decided the best time to learn was when babysitting "a friend's toddler." Much as the Tubbies watch children on their tummies even as children watch the Tubbies, babysitting Birtley watched the child watching the show: "The transformation in the little girl was amazing. A regular *Teletubbies* viewer, she danced to the theme tune, knew the names and loved watching the little film." Echoing one of Davenport's astute defenses, she pointedly asks, "What harm can a half-hour show do that limits its bad language to an "Oh-oh!" and its sex and violence to a group hug and a quick ride on Po's scooter?"

Chapter 5

Major Hit... Major Change

THE CONTROVERSY SWIRLING AROUND the show and its alleged "dumbing down" of kids' TV did not prevent *Teletubbies* from enchanting its intended audience of pre-school children and becoming a major hit. Indeed, it was not long before the show averaged two million viewers in Great Britain per episode.

Although its primary audience was always its intended audience—children in the ages one to four or five—*Teletubbies* attracted many other viewers as well. An article published in a July 1997 issue of *The Independent* by Vanessa Thorpe reported that the Teletubbies "have conquered the nation's toddlers and now they are taking the rave scene and the nation's students by storm." That article elaborated that there had been a music festival close to the *Teletubbies* location and, during that event, "several ravers attempted to break in and tread the hallowed turf. What is more, club DJs have dubbed the soundtrack on to dance mixes and the series is already the subject of a trendy Internet page."

John Simmit recalled being surprised by how big the show got. "I don't think anyone knew what a phenomenon *Teletubbies* would become," he said. "You become an attachment to the whirlwind. But as a grounded Jamaica-Brummies, I continued producing theater shows, DJing, and doing stand-up as the show exploded." For readers unfamiliar with the term "Brummies," it is used for people who hail from the city of Birmingham in England. As observed in a previous section of this book, "Brum" is a nickname for Birmingham.

Simmit was far from the only person working on the program to be surprised by its remarkable success. "The media interest astonished us all that first summer in 1997," Davenport recalled. Workers on the program were frequently discomfited by the sight of helicopters in the sky and Land Rovers driving toward the *Teletubbies* set.

One person who was *not* surprised by the success of the show was Nikky Smedley. "I thought, 'it will be massive,'" she recalled. "It came from a place of love and engagement for young children."

Another person who expected it would be a hit from the start was Dave Thompson. "In the early stages of filming, there was a euphoric atmosphere on set," he remembers. "The producers had done much research based on the previous TV shows they made for very young children so we knew the show was going to make a huge impact on TV throughout the world. All four of us cast stayed in the same hotel for much of the shooting and we socialized together in the evenings."

Along with being a super-hit with the public came official recognition from respected organizations. Royal Television Society nominated Ragdoll for BBC Education/Children's Entertainment for the *Teletubbies* episode "Playing in the Rain" for its RTS Educational Television Awards 1997 in the category Pre School & Infants. That same *Teletubbies* episode, "Playing in the Rain," won The Japan Prize for 1997. *Teletubbies* also won the 1997 Birmingham International Film and Television Award.

The media attention to *Teletubbies*, as well as the airing of the show, were sharply interrupted with the tragic car accident death of 36-year-old Princess Diana on August 31, 1997. The United Kingdom was plunged into grief by the death of this beloved figure—a grief shared throughout much of the world. Small children, not yet able to grasp the importance of Princess Diana or even the meaning of death, were upset that their favorite show was not being shown, with many confused UK toddlers asking parents and other caregivers, "Why aren't *Teletubbies* on?"

Teletubbies would return to the screen after the paroxysm of mourning ended. However, one of its major stars, Dave Thompson, was soon to receive some very unwelcome and painful news.

Tears of a Tinky Winky

A major change in *Teletubbies* casting was made at the end of the first season: Dave Thompson was terminated from his job as Tinky Winky.

It was the last day of filming for that season and the end of that particular day's filming. A wrap party was about to be held. Thompson was getting out of the Tinky Winky costume when informed he was fired. The previously mentioned article in the *Independent* quotes Thompson as remarking, "I was officially asked to leave in a letter from an accountant just before everyone else went off to the end of shooting wrap party."

He told this author, "I felt the timing was insensitive and when I told the others that I wasn't going to the party but was going to drive home to London, I broke into tears."

Thompson informed this interviewer that he is unclear as to the reasons why he was dismissed. He continued that Anne Wood decided he was to be fired. "The letter she sent me said they thought my behavior was professional and I had given the part my 'best shot,'" he elaborated. "It went on to say that my 'interpretation of the role had not been accepted.'" The Thorpe piece reported that he stated, "I wasn't given any clues as to what I was doing wrong." That same article reported, "In retrospect he suspects his voice may have been part of the problem. 'The other Teletubbies used their own voices but mine was dubbed over.'" As mentioned in the previous chapter, it is likely dissatisfaction with Thompson's voice that led to the hiring of Mark Heenehan to do Tinky Winky's lines.

It is important to add that neither Dave Thompson's life nor his career was ruined by this setback. In the years since his time as Tinky

Winky, Thompson has appeared on *Screech Owls* in 2002, on *Time Gentlemen Please* from 2000 to 2002, on an episode of *Blessed* in 2005, on *Huge* in 2010, on *TV Burp* from 2004 through 2012 and on *The Harry Hill Movie* in 2013. He has been a writer for *TV Burp* and *The Sketch Show* as well as pursuing a busy career as a stand-up comic.

Moreover, even though he no longer played Tinky Winky in new sketches after the first season, Thompson's presence continued on *Teletubbies*. "While I worked on the show we shot most of the generic shots that were used in all of the episodes," he states. "As a result, I appear in every episode they made, my name is in the credits, and I was on the payroll." He had worked on 70 episodes and definitely left his mark on *Teletubbies*.

The dismissal of Thompson caused distress in at least some *Teletubbies* fans. *The Radio Times* published the following letter expressing that distress.

> We are writing this letter in response to various media reports that the actor who plays Tinky Winky in *Teletubbies* has been sacked. We feel that altering the original cast will only be detrimental to the quality of the show; *Teletubbies* is one of the best children's shows since *Pigeon Street* and *Bagpuss*.
>
> As you can probably guess, we are not in the age group that *Teletubbies* is aimed at. We are aged 16-19, and among the large student following that the show has built up.
>
> Tinky Winky is an essential element of the Teletubby posse. To replace him would be like replacing Geri from the Spice Girls. No one could ever wield a handbag or sport a tutu like Tinky Winky.
>
> Georgina, Sophie and Fiona Clark Royston, Hertfordshire.

The Radio Times wrote back to reassure the young ladies: "Don't panic! Although the actor who played him may have changed, Tinky Winky is alive and well in Teletubbyland."

Indeed he was. Simon Shelton was cast as the new Tinky Winky. Shelton was a classically trained ballet dancer, choreographer, and actor. Prior to taking over the purple suit with the triangle antenna, Shelton had acted in a small part in the 1988 film *Anna,* played a male prostitute in the 1991 TV movie *Prisoner of Honor,* worked as a featured dancer in *Swing Kids* in 1993 and played "The Dark Knight" in the 1994 children's television series *Incredible Games*. There may be something a bit jarring in Shelton's having gone from playing a male prostitute in a film to playing parts in two children's series but it should be remembered that an actor plays *characters* so it is not uncommon to see an actor portray a murderer and then a police officer, a swinger and then a saint, a genius and then a mentally challenged person. In fact, being able to act in extremely divergent roles and make the characterizations effective and believable is a major feather in a performer's cap.

Apparently Shelton enjoyed the widespread adulation that so much of the public had for the Teletubbies. An article in *The Telegraph* reported that Shelton commented that playing a Teletubby was "like being a member of the Beatles." Indeed, the Teletubbies were often compared to the Beatles and, for many people, the Teletubbies were a modern day "Fab Four."

Teletubby Treats and Toys/Ragdoll is the Rage

As Christmas 1997 approached, Teletubby dolls were the most demanded items in stores throughout the United Kingdom. Parents, aunts, uncles, and others knew that the toddlers in their lives craved reproductions of Tinky Winky, Dipsy, Laa-Laa, and Po. However, as an article in the *BBC News* reported, by early November 1997, "Some shops have already rationed Teletubby dolls to one per customer." The same article noted that one million Teletubby dolls had been manufactured although, by the time of its early November writing, "only 300,000 had reached shops."

The *Irish Times* reported that people stood and waited in long lines to purchase Teletubby dolls as "the cuddly foursome lived up to predictions that they would be the number one Christmas toy this year [of 1997]." Approximately one million Teletubby dolls were sold by Christmas Day 1997.

A piece in *The Telegraph* observed, "Teletubbies merchandise, including books, dolls and baby clothes, proved so popular for the Christmas of 1997 that it outsold all other toys twice over."

With extraordinary popularity came an award in recognition of the place that Teletubby dolls had as merchandise. The *Toy Retailers Association* publication, a magazine that calls itself "The Voice for Toy Retailers in the UK & Ireland," noted that *Teletubbies* won the British Association of Toy Retailer's (BATR) Toy of the Year 1997/1998. The award was presented at the Royal Lancaster Hotel in London, England on February 1st, 1998 before an audience of roughly 600 people. The toy company that won the award was Golden Bear. David Fogel, BATR Chair, stated, "In an industry dominated by powerful multi-national companies, I am delighted that our award has been won by a family-run British toy company, Golden Bear in Telford, with toys based on a British television program."

Ragdoll Productions was catapulted into a whole new league as a result of the extraordinary success of *Teletubbies*. In an interview with reporter Anna Tims, "The series threw our company into a bigger arena," Wood commented. "From then on, there was the stress of trying to follow up the success, but art is not a factory."

TELETUBBIES TRAVELS

The British hit program was released in many countries outside its homeland. An article in *The Independent* by Paul McCann published in August 1997, only five months after the show's debut, noted that it had "already been sold to Portugal, France, and South Africa." McCann elaborated that some international program buyers "had a hard time understanding the characters, who have aerials on their heads and television screens on their screens in their stomachs." Head of sales for BBC Worldwide John Morris recalled that a buyer from Germany expressed fear that the Teletubbies "are like spacemen and we think they'll frighten our children." However, those fears were proved baseless by the small children themselves who were enchanted by the Teletubbies. Thus, it was not long before small children throughout Europe, the Middle East, Asia, both North and South America, Australia, and New Zealand were enjoying the wholesome antics of the brightly colored space babies whose trademark saying was "Big hug!"

Teletubbies made its way across the pond to the United States where it was distributed by Itsy Bitsy Entertainment and had its debut broadcast on the Public Broadcasting System (PBS)/PBS Kids on April 6, 1998.

The PBS version of the show had its own American narrator, actor Rolf Saxon. Why did Saxon get the job? "I was auditioned at the studio but as to why I was chosen… they liked my voice?"

Saxon estimates that he narrated "about 350 episodes." He has positive recollections of his work on the show. "It was actually a really enjoyable job," he says. "I'd done very little 'voice work' and nothing for children's TV up to that time so, although it was something of a learning curve for me, there was nothing challenging in a negative way at all as far as the voicing of the episodes. There was a very skilled and professional team on board and Anne Wood and Andrew Davenport had very carefully, over a number of years, crafted and created the show with a very strict set of parameters aimed at a very specific audience." Saxon thought the people with whom he worked were "a great team" and found it "genuinely a joy to come to work." He acknowledged one challenge: "Sometimes keeping a straight face while speaking the dialogue could be difficult."

Overall, what does Saxon think is the best thing about this series? "I think the fact that it achieved exactly what it set out to do: to educationally entertain very young children in a safe, fun, and nurturing way," he answers. "That sounds kind of trite and maybe even cliché but that's exactly—even now—what it still feels like to me."

Within two years of *Teletubbies*' debut, the show was being aired in well over 100 nations and translated into more than 40 languages. Like the German buyer who expressed reservations about the "space" look of the Tubbies and the possibility they would frighten children, others harbored reservations about these unusual make-believe creatures. A *BBC News* article reported that the BBC itself, "which sells the television programme around the world, says international buyers were at first taken aback by the bizarre look of the [characters]. But they have been won over by the evidence that for children between one and four years old, it is compulsive viewing." Indeed, small children across the globe loved *Teletubbies* and it became a cherished part of early childhood throughout the world. There were also many adults in diverse cultures who found themselves charmed by the colorful, overgrown "space" toddlers.

Of course, viewers, like the Teletubbies themselves, were also interested in the "real" parts of this beautifully bizarre show. The tummy films continued showcasing the varied activities and adventures of people, especially children, on planet earth. For example, a January 1998 episode with the self-explanatory title "Irish Dancing" showcased the developing skills of child dancers from the Bennett's End Community Centre in Hemel Hempstead, England. Ann Butler was a teacher of the group that got a chance to shine on the hit show through fortuitous happenstance. "We did a display in Abbotts Langley [an English village] and were approached after the display to see if we were interested [in appearing on *Teletubbies*]," Butler related to this author.

The children developing dancing talents into dancing skills were indeed interested in being on the show—save one individual. "They wanted my youngest dancers and one that should have done it was too shy," Butler revealed. Another young dancer took the place of the young lady who opted out due to her reticence and "was just as good," Butler said.

How did the kids and their teacher prepare for the filming? "I was just doing what I do in class," Butler remarks. "I didn't need to act." But she and the kids *did* need to prepare for the rolling cameras. "The dancers were told what to say," Butler says. "I worked with the girls beforehand for about two weeks." Teacher Ann Butler enjoyed working on *Teletubbies* and so did her young students. "It was fun and a really exciting time for the dancers," she cheerfully asserts. "It was really good fun!"

Olivia.

Olivia with lamb.

Olivia with goat.

Neal Patel.

King Pleasure.

King Pleasure.

Rolf Saxon, Teletubbies Narrator.

Dave Thompson in front of the Teletubby Dome.

Crew sets up Teletubbies scene

Tinky Winky on the set.

Chapter 6

Controversy: Is Tinky Winky Gay?

EVEN AS *TELETUBBIES* REMAINED embroiled in a controversy about the baby talk of its characters, a second, and very different, controversy erupted.

Andy Medhurst, a lecturer in Media, Film, and Cultural Studies at the University of Sussex, and co-editor with Sally Munt of *Lesbian and Gay Studies: A Critical Introduction*, was happy about what he saw as a positive aspect of *Teletubbies*; he wrote a letter to *The Face*, a British magazine devoted to popular culture, with his observations on the program. That venue published his letter in July 1997. Medhurst cheerfully wrote that Tinky Winky "may be the first queer role model for toddlers."

Only a few days after the Medhurst epistle saw the light of day, *The Guardian* published an article in which Tinky Winky was described as "a gay icon who prances around in a particularly campy way."

Although the target audience for *Teletubbies* was always small children, it also had viewers among the older teenagers and young adults who were part of the "raver" nightclub scene. Many of these fans, especially those in the LGBT community, happily latched onto the idea that Tinky Winky was gay. "When the show was originally transmitted, it was around six in the morning, when parents are getting up with their young children," Dave Thompson recalled in an interview with this author. "The show was also watched by ravers who were returning from nightclubs at around that time in the morning. Tinky Winky was adopted as a gay icon by gay clubbers."

When *Teletubbies* crossed the pond to North America in 1998, the question of Tinky Winky's "gayness" followed. *The Washington Post* hailed Tinky Winky as the "new Ellen Degeneres." *The Advocate*, one of the oldest and most esteemed magazines of the LGBT community, joyfully proclaimed, "Tinky Winky comes across as a big fabulous fag" and gushed, "He's become a gay icon" and predicted that "fundamentalists" would "flip when they see him."

A major fundamentalist did indeed flip. Rev. Jerry Falwell, one of the most respected and best known conservative Christian activists in the world, let his displeasure about Tinky Winky be known to the public in February 1998 in the *National Liberty Journal*, a magazine connected with the university Rev. Falwell founded. His piece was titled "Parent Alert: Tinky Winky Comes Out of the Closet." The anti-gay minister saw Tinky Winky as a gay character for precisely the same reasons his opponents saw the Tubby as a gay character: "He is purple—the gay pride color; and his antenna is shaped like a triangle—the gay pride symbol; he flaunts a red purse." Unlike his opponents, he viewed this as ominous, writing, "As a Christian, I feel that [Tinky Winky's] role modeling of the gay lifestyle is damaging to the moral lives of children." Only days after the issue of the *National Liberty Journal* with this essay was published, Rev. Falwell appeared on NBC's *Today* show to elaborate. He told Katie Couric, "To have little boys running around with purses and acting effeminate, and leaving the idea that the masculine male, the feminine female is out, and gay is O.K.—that's something Christians do not agree with."

Articles speculating on the sexual orientation of Tinky Winky appeared in newspapers and magazines; the question was discussed on radio and TV shows. Although Rev. Falwell was widely ridiculed for seeing Tinky Winky as gay, it should be said in fairness to him that gay activists were the first to make that connection. It should also be noted that the conservative Christian minister showed he did not lack a sense of humor as he often posed with Tinky Winky dolls, showing he did not fear the presence of his purple and triangle-antennaed nemesis.

There was a problem at the root of the speculation that was missed by both those who wanted Tinky Winky to be a "gay role model" and those who feared that he was one. Homosexuality is, of course, a *sexual* orientation—and the Teletubbies were fictional characters, fictional beings, who were deliberately created *without* sexuality of any kind.

It is true that both Tinky Winky's color and his antennae shape are popularly associated with gayness. But those things do not make him gay any more than the absence of them make Laa-Laa, Dipsy, and Po straight. All four Teletubbies are asexual fictional beings living in a fantasy world specifically created for pre-schoolers.

Sooooo... Mr. Davenport, what *about* that red handbag that Tinky Winky likes to carry? "Children get to a stage where they are fascinated by volume, and how things fit into other things," he observed. "A mother's handbag is fascinating to both genders because of all the precious objects kept inside." There was more than a touch of exasperation in Davenport's assertion: "Older children get the joke that it's being carried by a boy, but Tinky Winky wasn't supposed to the Archbishop of Canterbury, for God's sake. He was always supposed to be a bit silly."

Teletubbies producer for the United States, Kenn Viselman, also showed exasperation when he commented, "We're talking about a show for one to four-year-olds. If we had homosexuals in it, they wouldn't even know it—but for the record, we don't. Tinky Winky is simply a sweet, technological baby with a magic bag." He also observed, "This ridiculous question—'Is Tinky Winky a heterosexual or a homosexual?'—became the second largest story in the world. Literally the only story that got more global [attention] was Monica Lewinsky and her blue dress." The latter referred to President Bill Clinton's unfortunate extramarital liaison with a White House intern, a relationship which, together with his lying about it, led to his impeachment, although not his removal, from office.

Itsy Bitsy Entertainment spokesperson Steve Rice commented, "The fact that [Tinky Winky] carries a magic bag doesn't make him gay. It's a children's show, folks. To think we would be putting sexual innuendo into a children's show is kind of outlandish. To 'out' a Teletubby in a pre-school show is kind of sad on his part. I really find it absurd and kind of offensive." Rev. Falwell retorted that he found these explanations "disingenuous and insufficient."

Although some members of the LGBT community had already adopted Tinky Winky as a gay symbol, the backlash instigated by Rev. Falwell made this adoption even more popular. There was talk of Tinky Winky being Grand Marshal in the 1999 San Francisco Gay Pride Parade. (Harry Hay was the actual Grand Marshal for that year).

Nikky Smedley believes adults should not project their own issues on media made specifically for children and thinks it foolish to see gay innuendo in *Teletubbies*. "I think it's embarrassing for the people who said it," she asserted. "What kind of person can take the obvious innocence and turn it into something else? We were hardly sexual beings."

In an interview with this author, Dave Thompson backed up the contention that the question of gayness or straightness is simply inapplicable. "The Teletubbies are asexual beings," he comments. "They have gender but they don't have sexuality or genitals. They are for very young children who deserve to have their childhood. Adults projected adult sexuality onto the characters." Thompson also believes grown-ups projected inappropriate meanings onto Tinky Winky's special prop. "Tinky Winky carries a red handbag, or purse, in American [English usage]," Thompson observes. "Each Teletubby has a favorite toy: Po has the scooter, Laa-Laa has the ball, Dipsy has the hat, and Tinky Winky has the handbag. They are all found objects which the Teletubbies use without understanding their meaning. Tinky Winky has no awareness that his handbag was designed for a woman." Thompson further states, "There's no sexuality conveyed by the Teletubbies because they're pre-sexual beings created to entertain very young children. They have gender but not sexuality."

There was some public speculation that Thompson had been fired because he brought an element to his portrayal of Tinky Winky that led to the perception of the character as homosexual. Journalist Charlotte Runcie wrote, "It has been claimed that the production company, Ragdoll, felt [Dave Thompson] was 'misinterpreting' the role by implying Tinky Winky was gay." An article by Robin Edds that appears on Buzzfeed.com asserts that Thompson "was reportedly removed from the show after he gave an interview in which he admitted to playing the character as a homosexual." However, Thompson adamantly insisted to the author of this book that no such interview ever took place. "I never said I interpreted the role of Tinky Winky as a homosexual," he maintains. "Somebody made that statement up and wrongly attributed it to me." Thompson also told this author that there was nothing of himself that he could have put in the character that should lead to the perception of Tinky Winky as homosexual. "I am personally not gay," he says. "I have an ex-wife and two daughters."

Thompson's replacement in the purple suit, Simon Shelton, was similarly dismissive of the idea that Tinky Winky was gay. Shelton said he found the entire controversy "amusing and quite staggering" and wondered, "Is it for real?" Oddly, Shelton was unfamiliar with the famous Rev. Jerry Falwell prior to the controversy. "I didn't know who he was and thought it was someone trying to become famous," Shelton related. Of course, Rev. Falwell had long been world famous and enjoyed a large following of supporters.

Interestingly, writer Ruth Graham published an essay in *Slate* in 2017 in which she revisited the controversy and supported the contention that Tinky Winky was meant to be a gay character. She wrote, "To call Tinky Winky 'gay' does not mean Tinky Winky has sex, and the mere presence of queer characters is not in itself 'sexual innuendo.' It is now much more widely understood than it was in the '90s that sexuality and gender expression may emerge long before sexual maturity." Graham believes that Tinky Winky's "gay" characteristics were to be applauded as they indicated that "children's television—and culture in general—was becoming much more comfortable with queerness.

Although the controversy about the supposed sexuality of a fictional character who was in fact created as asexual may have been a classic case of "Much Ado About Nothing;" it did not negatively impact the show's popularity. The show continued to gain loyal fans and bring joy to children throughout the world.

Panic in Poland

Years after its 2001 cancellation, *Teletubbies* continued to be seen in re-runs throughout the world. In 2007, the country of Poland was the setting of a controversy over the allegedly gay sexual orientation of Tinky Winky.

It should be noted that Poland in the mid-2000s was not a country friendly to the LGBT community. The European Union (EU), together with various human rights groups, had criticized the Polish government's policies regarding LGBT people. A May 2007 *Sydney Morning Herald* article reported, "Polish Education Minister Roman Giertych has proposed laws sacking teachers who promote 'homosexual lifestyle' and banning 'homo-agitation' in schools."

During this same period, Ewa Sowinska was Children's Rights Ombudsman for Poland. Her investigation was prompted, at least in part, by the Teletubby's special item. "I noticed he has a lady's purse—but I didn't realize he's a boy," she commented in a magazine interview. "At first I thought the purse would be a burden for this Teletubby." Indeed, when stunt coordinator Tom Delmar played Tinky Winky, he found it a burden when doing stunts. She elaborated, "Later I learned that this may have a homosexual undertone."

Sowinska began putting the question of Tinky Winky's possible negative role modeling to "top child psychologists" in Poland. However, she had not pursued the question for long before announcing her findings to the media. She declared, "The opinion of a leading sexologist, who maintained that this series has no negative effects on a child's psychology, is perfectly credible; as a result, I have decided that it is no longer necessary to seek the opinion of other psychologists."

However, there were critics who found fault with the conclusions of the experts Sowinska consulted. In further press interviews, she stated, "They are fictional characters, they have nothing to do with reality." She continued, "The bag… and other props the fictional characters use are there to create a fictional world that speaks to children."

Teletubbies continued to be seen in Poland. The four furry creatures became cherished childhood memories for Poles. Sadly, the same could not be said for the young of Kazakhstan where the show was reportedly banned by the personal order of the President because of the suspicion that Tinky Winky "was a sex pervert."

Po the Potty-Mouthed Homophobe?

Although it never garnered the attention paid to the issue of whether or not Tinky Winky was gay, questions of an opposite sort were expressed about Po—or, rather, about talking Po dolls. Some people heard a bigoted message aimed at male homosexuals in the high-pitched baby talk of the little red Teletubby. There were also people who said such dolls made graphic sexual overtures.

When people pushed the doll's belly to make it talk, they thought she said, "Faggot, faggot." Some people thought she said, "Fatty, fatty." What the doll actually said was the Cantonese term, "Fi-dit, fi-dit," which means, "Faster, faster." Some people also thought they heard the toy say, "Bite my butt" when it was saying gibberish that actress Pui Fan Lee based on Cantonese. Charlotte Runcie wrote in *The Telegraph* that "shops in Texas pulled" the plush Po dolls because customers complained about Po's supposedly foul and/or bigoted mouth. An October 1988 *Associated Press* piece by Katie Fairbank stated, "But toymaker Hasbro, which manufactures the stuffed doll, started earlier this month inserting language cards in each doll's box to familiarize people with the Teletubby language." That same article reported that an Itsy Bitsy Entertainment Company spokesperson, Eileen Potluck, stated, "Each Teletubby has its own gibberish" and that "a lot of people are buying the dolls because they're cute and they're not familiar with the series." Unfamiliarity with the series, she seemed to suggest, could lead to major misinterpretations.

Fairbank's article also reported that a four-store chain called Arlington Toy Enterprises "pulled the Po dolls off its shelves and sent them back to Hasbro." Dean May, Arlington Toy Enterprises President, explained, "We were just trying to head off any potential problems. It is very difficult to discern what that one was saying."

Awards

Just as the "dumbing down" controversy failed to "down" the success of *Teletubbies*, the furor over Tinky Winky's supposed sexual orientation failed to dampen the enthusiasm of the public for the delightful series. The popular show also continued to garner special honors for its work on behalf of the little ones. The series was nominated for an Emmy award in the category Outstanding Pre-school Children's Series 1998-1999.

Teletubbies won the Educational Television Awards 2000 of the Royal Television Society for its episode "Scrapbook" in the category Pre School & Infants.

In November 2000, the Children's section of the British Academy of Film and Television Art (BAFTA) honored Anne Wood with a special award for what the *BBC News* described as her "outstanding contribution to television." *Teletubbies* itself was nominated for an award in the Pre-School Live Action category.

Long after its cancellation, the show continued to be honored. In 2014, *Teletubbies* won Best Non-Fiction Programme of the last 50 Years and Greatest Impact Programme of the last 50 Years from the prestigious Prix Jeunesse, an international organization that bills itself as "dedicated to promoting excellence in children's TV."

Chapter 7

Tubby Bye-Bye

EVEN AS CONTROVERSIES ERUPTED and faded, *Teletubbies* continued, the sprightly Tubbies enjoying the peculiar pleasures and simple adventures available to them in Teletubbyland. Laa-Laa danced with her ball, Dipsy played with his hat, Po raced around on her scooter, and Tinky Winky put things into and took them out of his magic bag. The Tubbies fell down and laughed as they fell down, bumped tummies, frolicked, played varied versions of hide and seek, and gave each other "big hugs." In various episodes, the Tubbies competed to see who would eat Tubby Custard the slowest, Noo-Noo raced around the Teletubby House vacuuming up this and that and sometimes spewing the items out again, the Tubbies tried gymnastics, Tinky Winky danced on the roof, and a Voice Trumpet cheekily pretended to be a Gingerbread Man.

There was one episode in which the Teletubbies watched a film about children discovering things that are green; Tinky Winky, Laa-Laa, and Po find different green things in Teletubbyland but all three decide that their favorite green item is—what else?—Dipsy. In other episodes the Tubbies danced a conga, watched a film about an elephant being washed, and stood under a cloud until it started raining. The Tubbies viewed a film in which a young girl painted a portrait of her Dad, another in which boys played with piglets, and still another in which children baked bread. The Tubbies were visited by Little Bo Peep and her lamb. The Teletubbies watched a little girl playing with a toy farm, kids creating mosaics from different shapes, kids learning about caterpillars, and saw children winding up a clockwork robot. There were episodes in which the Tubbies watched a child pretending to fly to the moon, a kid painting a picture of a turkey, and children searching for shrimp in rock pools. They saw children gazing at the moon through a telescope and watched a child make drawings with chalk. The Teletubbies learned beloved nursery rhymes like "How Now Brown Cow." They learned about ladybirds, yoga, circles, seahorses, fox cubs, badgers, ducks, bagels, chameleons, pianos, elephants, gardens, llamas, and goats. There were episodes about Indian saris, seals, puppies, fish, monkeys, obstacle courses, cricket, and rickshaws. Other things explored on this delightful show were floating and squeezing, hanging out the wash, and blowing bubbles.

Describing the plots of the events in Teletubbyland as well as those in the "Tummy Tales" can lead many people to shrug and frown at their banality. Such people need to be reminded that, for the target audience of this show, *everything is new* since they have only recently entered the world. Things that are ordinary and common to adults, or even to older children, can fascinate small children and be experienced as exciting adventures. *Teletubbies* was made for small children and that audience found it enthralling.

The young audience that watched *Teletubbies* was made up of children throughout the world. As a *BBC News* article published in March 1999 noted, "Since their debut in 1997, the Teletubbies have mutated into a massive children's television phenomenon and rights to the show have been sold in every corner of the globe." That same piece observes that the show raked in 23 million pounds for BBC Worldwide in 1998. What's more, while *Teletubbies* became a treasured part of the childhoods of young children, it continued to also attract grown-up viewers who were either watching with the children for whom they cared or just liked the program for its inspired combination of silliness and love, the latter beautifully exemplified by its trademark slogan, "Big hug!" *Teletubbies* had the distinction of being BBC Worldwide's biggest export.

However, even good things—even *very* good things—come to an end. By their very nature, television shows do not go on forever. *Teletubbies* was cancelled in 2001 with its final episode—one about blowing bubbles—airing on February 16, 2001.

There had been no less than 365 episodes of the groundbreaking TV show for the youngest possible audience. It had been exported to over 120 nations and translated into 45 languages.

After its cancellation, *Teletubbies* did not, of course, disappear from the airwaves as re-runs were shown and continue to be shown to the day of this writing in 2019. Over a billion children worldwide had watched the activities of Teletubbyland, as well as the adventures of real children from the Teletubby tummy films, and the show continues to enthrall, amuse, and educate the youngest of the young all over the globe. Even after its cancellation, the show continued generating money for the BBC. As a *Guardian* piece published in 2006 reported, by that year it had contributed no less than 120 million pounds "from overseas sales and merchandise to the BBC's coffers."

A Deliberate Flood, A Study, and Good Works Galore

To at least one individual, the cancellation of *Teletubbies* was a relief. Farmer Rosemary Harding was royally sick of the attention the filming of the show garnered to her land. Thus, after its cancellation, Harding decided to make a major change to the land that had served the public so admirably as Teletubbyland. "People were jumping fences and crossing cattle fields," Harding recalled. When the filming of *Teletubbies* stopped, she commented, "We're glad to see the back of it." Thus, she had the lovely green area flooded and transformed into a pond. She turned what had been Teletubbyland into an aquatics center.

Although the show stopped making new episodes, it continued to be viewed worldwide on TV channels and YouTube. After all, as previously noted, it was several years after the show was cancelled that a controversy about Tinky Winky's supposed gayness erupted in Poland.

In 2007, a study was done on the vexing question of *Teletubbies* and language acquisition. It is unlikely anyone was surprised that the study found that Tinky Winky, Dipsy, Laa-Laa, and Po could not take the place of real life grown-ups in teaching children to talk. Researchers at Wake Forest University in North Carolina of the United States found, as a *Reuters* article stated, "Babies learn their first words better from people than the popular television characters." Wake Forest University Associate Professor of Communication Marina Krcmer remarked, "With the tremendous success of programs such as *Teletubbies* that target very young children, it has become important to understand what very young children are taking away from these programs." The study found, "Children younger than 22 months old could not link an object to a new word when it was presented on the program but they were able to make the connection when an adult in the same room taught them the word." The *Reuters* piece continued that studies have proven that children who are three years of age or older can learn language from TV shows. However, there was no real conflict between the conclusions of the study and the beliefs of those who created *Teletubbies* since, as reported in Chapter 4 of this book, Andrew Davenport observed, "Children learn to speak from the continuous real world and real people around them; a half-hour TV program is not going to affect that."

The extraordinary success of *Teletubbies* enabled Wood to set up the Ragdoll Foundation in 2001. The Ragdoll website states, "In the early days of the company, Anne's cold calling on US broadcasters and distributors became legendary. She was always received with polite respect for the modest Ragdoll catalogue but the enthusiasm was never transformed into deals until *TotsTV*, with its unique ability to feature a second language, and *Teletubbies* were both shown on the PBS network." That same year of 2001, Anne Wood ranked third wealthiest individual in British broadcasting with that enormous wealth due in large part to *Teletubbies*. The prominent British magazine *Broadcast* estimated her company's value as 130 million pounds. She cheerfully acknowledged that the series bought her business "a big influx of money—far more than we had previously had."

Widespread knowledge of Wood's riches led many organizations to request her help. Wanting to help in a focused and systematic manner, she created the Ragdoll Foundation.

The good works of the Ragdoll Foundation have been many and varied but a common thread runs through them in the founder's special interest in children. For example, in 2004, the Ragdoll Foundation launched Women's Aid Listening to Children, a campaign in which children who had suffered because of domestic violence crafted drawings and made statements that were put on postcards. These postcards were sent to the United Kingdom's then-Minister for Children, Margaret Hodge, in the hopes of persuading the government to give greater support to children's concerns around domestic violence.

Andrew Davenport also went on to other projects. He came up with the idea for the popular Ragdoll Productions TV series *In the Night Garden...* (2007-2008), a BBC children's series featuring colorful puppet characters enjoying adventures in a magical garden, and wrote the scripts for its 100 episodes as well as writing its title theme and incidental music. He created and was producer for the TV series *Tronji* (2009), a Ragdoll Productions show commissioned by CBBC.

A Telltale Test and a Bright "British Invasion"

That *Teletubbies* entered the culture of the United Kingdom in a major way can be seen by the report made by the *Daily Mail* in 2002 that candidates for the Metropolitan Police's Special Branch were asked to name the Teletubbies in an entrance exam. Test takers who failed to name Tinky Winky, Dipsy, Laa-Laa, and/or Po lost points on that exam. Apparently, it was believed that familiarity with the Tubbies was an index of a British person's knowledge of his or her popular culture.

Simon Shelton, Nikky Smedley, John Simmit, and Pui Fan Lee occasionally donned their Tubby suits even after the show was no longer filming new episodes. For example, in 2007, the four performers traveled to New York City for a 10th anniversary celebration of *Teletubbies*. NYC Mayor Michael Bloomberg officially declared March 28, 2007 as "Teletubbies Day." They wore their Teletubby costumes for events in the Big Apple including being presenting with the keys to the city by its mayor. A *Today* show compared the group to another group from the United Kingdom to which they had often been compared, saying, "The Teletubbies are borrowing a page from the Beatles, staging their own British Invasion.... They are catching the sights of New York City indulging Grand Central Station, the Apollo Theater, and the Statue of Liberty." Shelton, Smedley, Simmit, and Lee were out of costume for their *Today* show in-studio interview but reverted to Teletubby baby talk for part of it. The NYC based Ragdoll Productions office made a deal with famous fashion designer Isaac Mizrahi as part of celebrating the 10th anniversary of *Teletubbies*. An article by Gary Rusak archived in *Kidscreen* reported, "The deal includes the auctioning of Teletubbies-inspired bags designed by Mizrahi. The proceeds from the auction, to be held this spring, are earmarked for Cure Autism Now and Autism Speaks charities."

Teletubby Performers Post-*Teletubbies*

As previously noted, Dave Thompson enjoyed a very active and lucrative career after losing his Tinky Winky gig.

In 2001, Pui Fan Lee took a role that startled, and even upset, some observers. She played in a television drama entitled *Metrosexuality* in which she did a steamy lesbian love scene. She told an interviewer that she "didn't take the lesbian role to be deliberately controversial." Rather, Lee asserted, "Yes, I was Po but I'm an actress, too, and the role looked interesting, exciting, and challenging." Lee also played in the TV crime drama series *State of Play* (2003) and *M.I.T.: Murder Investigation Team* (2003-2005). As a presenter for CBeebies, she worked in shows about birthdays and would use her "Po voice" when a Teletubbies card was presented.

Nikky Smedley was director, producer, and choreographer for the Ragdoll Productions television series *Boohbah* (2003), an educational show designed to teach infants and toddlers such basic skills as simple counting and the identifying of colors. Her website relates that she "trains and coaches grown-ups in the arts of Storytelling, Puppetry and Creating for Children—as well as offering Conference Speaking and Business Development around effective communication skills." She teaches Pilates, a form of exercise. Smedley is Director of the organization "Changing Cultures" that bills itself as consisting of "experts in creativity and engagement."

John Simmit continued working as a stand-up comic. In 1992, he founded Upfront Comedy, a company that produces comic series in theaters in major UK cities. Reporter Poppy Brady noted in *The Voice* that Simmit is often "credited with putting black British comedy on the map." When Brady interviewed Simmit in a 2017 interview, Simmit said he still receives "humbling messages from fans in their twenties thanking you for making their childhood happy."

Sadly, the second Tinky Winky, Simon Shelton, suffered an untimely death. Early on the morning of January 17, 2017, he was found dead in Liverpool. He was 52 years old. An inquest found the cause of death was "misadventure" due to a "high concentration of alcohol" and the frigid temperatures in the area at the time. Coroner Anita Bhardwaj reported, "Simon Shelton was 52 with a medical history of alcohol dependence." Andrew Davenport sent a letter of condolence to the late actor's family in which Davenport wrote, "Simon was an extraordinary performer and a wonderful person" and stating, "He brought a singular joy to Tinky Winky, and to all of us."

Indeed, the joy of Tinky Winky, Laa-Laa, Dipsy, and Po is apt to be with "all of us" for a very, very long time.

Chapter 8

2015 Teletubbies Say Eh-oh Again!

IN 2013, ANNE WOOD AND ANDREW DAVENPORT sold the rights to *Teletubbies*, as well as Ragdoll Productions, to the Canadian company DHX Media for the sum of 17.4 million pounds.

In June 2014, the BBC announced that a reboot of *Teletubbies* would be created and aired on the CBeebies channel, a BBC owned and operated TV channel oriented toward children. The new episodes were ordered from DHX Media and would be created by the United Kingdom production company Darrall Macqueen.

When the plans for rebooting were made public, the generation that had loved and cherished *Teletubbies* 1997-2001 had grown into young adulthood. These cheeky twenty-somethings often had fun with their memories of the show. Stuart Heritage wittily observed in an April 2015 article about the upcoming reboot that the original series had become a "fixed point in time by which self-obsessed millennials could chart their gradual decay." Some of those millennials would tweet "Here's what the Sun Baby looks like now!" and then tweet a photograph "of Charlie Chaplin or Kim Jong-un or the screaming skull from the end of that Indiana Jones film."

At least one individual was not pleased that there would be a second *Teletubbies*. Anne Wood told reporters she was "a bit sad" about the reboot, partly because she believed it showed a reluctance to bring new visions to children's TV programming. "It comes down to the times we're in. People feel safer remaking hits of the past rather than investing in something new," she asserted. Wood added that she was disappointed that "such a lot" of children's shows were "being remade." She stated, "I just feel the children's television industry is worth more than that." Although she did not appreciate the rebooting, she had no power to stop it since she had sold the rights to the program.

DHX President Steven DeNure believed the second version of the show would benefit from ever advancing technology. "The last episodes were made in 2001 and technology has really changed dramatically," he commented. "The Teletubbies always had a relationship with tech for little kids—among other things a screen on their bellies and a vacuum cleaner as a best friend. It is a preschool show that has a very gentle introduction to technology in a relatively indirect way. We are updating them in beautiful HD episodes."

Cbeebies Controller Kay Benbow was certain the new series would, like its predecessor, be a big hit. "*Teletubbies* is an enduringly popular series with our youngest viewers, although no new episodes have been made for over ten years," Benbow observed. "Early development and test shoots have persuaded me that CBeebies viewers are in for a wonderful treat."

While the first version of *Teletubbies* was filmed outdoors, this *Teletubbies* reboot was filmed in a BBC studio, specifically at Twickenham Studios. An article in *Broadcast* reported, "In pre-production, the Teletubbies world was created as a CG (computer generated) model so that the VFX team could control the layout of the terrain and test the composition of the shots with director Jack Jameson and director of photography Simon Reay. . . Around 30 artists worked on the project for a year."

Ant Howells, the Production Designer on the second *Teletubbies*, believed the second *Teletubbies* benefitted from being essentially immune to climate changes. "The original *Teletubbies* was filmed in the countryside and the actual interior was the interior of the dome so they were very weather reliant," he told an interviewer.

"If it was raining they went inside and if it was sunny they went outside." Thus, he continues, if the weather was inhospitable, "The world of the *Teletubbies* wasn't sunny, wasn't bright, wasn't a glorious summer day." He pointed out that the second *Teletubbies* faced no such limitations. "By doing it as a model, we're in control of that," he said. "The landscape is all 3-D printed." Howell elaborated that the makers of the reboot took special care to get precisely what they wanted for the series. "We dress the model with some of the grass that had to be specially manufactured in Germany because we couldn't get the right color and the right texture [here]," he stated. "Then we have the flowers. We have four varieties—buttercups, poppies, daisies, and cornflowers—which were laser cut. Then we mixed them up with dried flowers that were handprinted as well to make them look more realistic and naturalistic." The Teletubbyland of the reboot boasted over 60,000 dried or handmade flowers.

The Creative Director for LOLA (a visual special effects company specializing in computer generated effects on live action) Teletubbies' Special Effects was Rob Harvey. "*Teletubbies* has been a fascinating project for us," he stated. "It's basically getting the *Teletubbies* live action full scale on a blue-screen to work on a model environment and then enhancing that model to fill it out, to be a full environment as the place where they live. On top of that, we're putting in CG flowers and trees and bubbles, all sorts of things, the magic from the windmill—all the little elements that make the *Teletubbies* the *Teletubbies*."

For readers unfamiliar with the technical side of filmmaking, the blue-screen is an evenly-lit, monochromatic background, usually of a blue or green color, before which actors perform. In post-production, the blue-screen background is replaced (matted) through techniques by which other footage or computer-generated images (CGI) form the background that is actually seen by viewers.

One result of the filming technique was that the world of the Teletubbies, always bright and colorful, seemed even a tad bit more colorful with its shades being sharper. For example, the second Sun

Baby's lips are slightly redder than those of the original Sun Baby.

Workers in the Prop Shop crafted a 3-D version of the model background. They filled that model with tree stumps and rabbit holes that prop workers individually planted and carved out along with synthetic grass and flowers. This elaborately crafted model was mounted on a turntable. Degrees were marked on the turntable so the right section could be quickly turned to the camera.

STARS

When the rebooting was announced, *The Telegraph* reported that the new *Teletubbies* would boast "an all-star cast"—and indeed it did.

Daniel Rigby, stand-up comedian and actor, was the narrator of the second *Teletubbies*. As a stand-up comic, he made a big splash at the Latitude Festival. He won the 2007 Laughing Horse New Act of the Year and was nominated for the 2007 So You Think You're Funny contest. He was hardly a stranger to television series work, having played Mr. Martin in *Big School* (2013-2014), Chris in *Undercover* (2015), and Charles Blackwood in *Jericho* (2016). He was delighted to be selected to narrate the *Teletubbies* reboot. "It was amazing because *Teletubbies* are a sort of national institution and it felt like a privilege," he asserted. He was also pleased to do even more for the new series: "I'm not just narrating the series, I'm also singing the theme tune—which is one of the best things that's ever happened to me."

Actress Rebecca Hyland was cast to don the yellow suit and sport an antenna that curls and then straightens as Laa-Laa. This performer was no stranger to children's programming as she had been Upsy Daisy of *In the Night Garden* (2007-2009). Dipsy of the green hue and completely straight antenna was to be played by Nick Wellington, another *In the Night Garden* veteran, having depicted Igglepiggle on that show. Again replicating the original, this Dipsy possessed a face noticeably darker than that of the other three Teletubbies. Rachelle Beinart would be little red Po with the soap bubble-style antenna. Prior to winning a part on the reboot, she had played Drum in *ZingZillas* (2011-2012). The actor who would be in purple and sport the triangle antenna was Jeremiah Krage who had been Zak in *ZingZillas*.

Several performers were enlisted as Voice Trumpets. One of them was Academy Award winner Jim Broadbent, a busy and distinguished actor who won his Oscar for Best Supporting Actor in the 2001 motion picture *Iris*. He was also famous for playing Horace E. F. Slughorn, teacher of potions, in the Harry Potter movies. "*Teletubbies* is truly a British institution and it's very exciting to be involved in bringing this global hit back to our TV screens," Broadbent said. "I'm really looking forward to working with the Teletubbies and giving them big hugs."

Rochelle Humes had played in the television shows *I Dream* (2004) and *Myths* (2009), and been in the violent, definitely-not-for-small-children British crime thriller *Big Fat Gypsy Gangster* (2011) before she was chosen to be a Voice Trumpet on the *Teletubbies* reboot. She relished being part of the enterprise at least in part because, as someone born in 1989, she was a member of what could be called "the *Teletubbies* generation." She had watched the show as a child and loved it. All grown up and the mother of a small child when the reboot was shot, she was pleased to contribute to a show with a positive message. "Everything the Teletubbies do is about play and all about fun and all about big hugs," Humes observed.

Another Voice Trumpet was David Walliams, a famous British actor, author, comic, talent show judge and TV presenter. He has acted in motion pictures like *Little Britain* (2003) and *Run, Fat Boy, Run* (2007) and entered living rooms as a judge on *Britain's Got Talent*. Of getting Voice Trumpet work, he states, "It's really thrilling to be asked to take part in *Teletubbies* because it's such an iconic show and it's watched all around the world by millions and millions of children," he gushed. "It's too good of a thing to turn down."

Actress Fearne Cotton was also a Voice Trumpet for the *Teletubbies* reboot. Like Rebecca Hyland, Cotton was a mother and, as was true with Hyland, that real life role helped make working on a children's show special to her. Even before the debut aired, Cotton remarked, "I think viewers are going to go absolutely crazy for the new *Teletubbies*. Obviously, historically it is an iconic brand, people know it and love it. You're going to get exactly what you want from *Teletubbies*, but 2015-style. There will be new elements in there, new surprises, things that will make your kids go crazy in a good way, stimulate them. It's going to be the sort of thing that will capture kids' imaginations and their attention and, as a mum, that is exactly what I want!"

THE FRESH AND NEW *TELETUBBIES* DEBUTS

In the reboot, a new Sun Baby opened the show. The baby's name was publicly given only as Berry. This Sun Baby possessed a narrower face than the first but was just as pretty and equally winsome when giggling and squealing.

Episode 1 of the *Teletubbies* reboot was first aired on November 9, 2015 and was entitled "Making Friends."

The first thing seen was the new Sun Baby rising over the bucolic greenery. There was a difference in that the sun's rays did not come to points as they did in the original show but appeared as long rectangles that came to straight, flat ends.

A domed house similar to the first is seen but instead of the sleek, neatly-manicured green roof, the roof is bulky with greenery and rippled with flowers. From a hole on top of the roof, the Tubbies jump out: Tinky Winky, Dipsy, Laa-Laa, and finally Po.

Rather than the title appearing to be made out of balloons, a yellow background shaped like the top of a mushroom appears with the word "Teletubbies" in blue print rimmed with pink.

The four brightly colored space babies run around the Voice Trumpets. The audience hears the enthusiastic cry, "Time for

Teletubbies! Time for Teletubbies!" Then follow Tubby introductions, each saying his or her name: "Tinky Winky!" "Dipsy!" "Laa-Laa!" "Po!" They bump tummies and have a trademark "Big hug."

The windmill appears but it is not the four-angled windmill of the original but a completely round device that is lined into "slices," rather like a pizza but the slices are rectangles rather than triangles.

Suddenly we just see the bucolic landscape and a Voice Trumpet asks, "Where have the Teletubbies gone?" Cut to the Sun Baby smiling.

Then to the Teletubbies—who are, of course, never gone for long in either the first show or this one. "One day in Teletubbyland, the Teletubbies all said 'Hello,'" the cheerful narrator announces. Then Tinky Winky says, "Eh-oh" to Dipsy who returns the greeting. The two bump tummies, making a loud "squeak" noise and then bump butts, making that same squeak. This is repeated with Dipsy and Laa-Laa and then Laa-Laa and Po. Since there is no one behind the line, to whom will Po say "Hello"? This is soon solved as Tinky Winky changes places to go to the end of the line.

The windmill turns: something will happen! The Teletubbies run around, fall down, and happily wave their arms and legs around as the busy windmill emits pink sparkles.

The Tubbies stand up and gather together. Antennas and tummy screens light up. The tummy screen that remains lit is that of Tinky Winky. This tummy screen has a large button in the shape of an arrow. Po presses that arrow and we are transported to the film that is set in the real world.

In the film, children are at school. They play with building blocks. The teacher asks kids to put on aprons which they do so they can make handprints with paint. The short film ends and we return to the Tubbies. "Again! Again!" say the Teletubbies and the film is shown a second time.

When the second showing of the short film finishes, we again return to Teletubbyland where the group of four Teletubbies walk in a ragged single file. The narrator states, "Po saw something." Po squeals and giggles. The narrator explains, "It was a flower!" Po says, "Fl —eh." Then Laa-Laa sees something—another flower. Then Dipsy sees something—a very large flower. Then Tinky Winky sees—no flower! However, a flower soon appears and then, as the narrator says, "There were lots and lots of flowers!" the Teletubbies happily look at the many flowers suddenly sprouting around them. "The Teletubbies love flowers and the Teletubbies love each other!" the narrator observes. The group has a trademark big hug.

Then we are told, "Time for Tubby bye-bye."

Each of the Teletubbies waves bye and vanishes into a hole. They pop up again but, *nooooo*, as in the original it *is* time for Tubby bye-bye and they disappear into a hole leading to the Teletubby Home.

As was true with the original, the debut of the second *Teletubbies* set the tone and stage for what followed. As in the original, many shots would be repeated in each episode. The opening and closing would be the same. Other things would remain familiar as the windmill's turning signaled something about to happen and the Teletubbies take joy in simple things including cheerful falls and big hugs. The Teletubbies would appear, disappear from view, and a Voice Trumpet would ask, "Where have the Teletubbies gone?" Each Teletubby in the reboot had the same toy as in the original: Tinky Winky had the bag, Dipsy had the hat, Laa-Laa had the ball, and Po had her scooter.

Humes enjoyed her work on the show, at least in part because she knew she did a good job. "I guess my role is trying to bring the fun," Humes remarks. "I like to think I'm quite good at that." She elaborates, "I don't think I change my voice that much—just a happier, more cheerful, fun version of myself."

In an interview about his work on the reboot, Broadbent asserted, "It's one of the strangest and most satisfying jobs I've done. I've played quite a lot of inanimate objects, I've played vegetables, pigeons, and robots. I was even a talking lavatory seat. I think the Voice Trumpet work is quite special."

Walliams thought the second *Teletubbies* visually benefited from advances in cinematic science: "It looks incredible because technology has moved on so much, but it stayed completely true to the spirit of the original series."

ATTRACTIONS NEW AND NOVEL

While the *Teletubbies* reboot was indeed "completely true to the spirit of the original series," there were innovations. Some of these fresh things were slight. The screens on the tummies now boasted big arrows that another Tubby pressed to get the short film started. Noo-Noo, the peculiarly charming combination vacuum cleaner and pet with the big round eyes, is in the reboot. However, the body of the reboot Noo-Noo is not colored bright blue, as it was in the original, but is in shades of orange and pink.

Another innovation is in the way the Tubbies come into their domed home. In the first, they go down a slide; in the second, they are taken into their home via a round elevator called the "Dup-Dup."

Some brand new items were more significant. "There's lots of new additions, one of them being the Hidey Hup which is a like a big playground," Humes relates. "There's a big slide, a seesaw, a roundabout, and a trampoline. The way the Tubbies get there is in the Tubby Car."

The Tubby Car is first seen in Season 2 in the episode "Honk Honk." The short film in the episode is of kids in a car museum delightedly honking automobile horns. Back in Teletubbyland, the Tubby Car, a vehicle with four seats *and* four driving wheels, appears. The Teletubbies each get into a seat and behind a driving wheel. As they drive, the narrator sings a line of a song and the Teletubbies sing it back: "Vroom vroom, honk honk, drive along/ Vroom vroom, honk honk, drive along/Vroom vroom, honk honk, sing a song/Vroom vroom, honk honk, sing a song/And stop!"

The Hidey Hup is also introduced in the second season, in an episode that is aired shortly after "Honk Honk." The episode in which a first trip to the Hidey Hup is taken is "Spinning." After the second showing of a short film about children spinning tops around, the Teletubbies are seen in their Tubby Car. First, the Tubby Car spins round and round. Then it heads for the Hidey Hup that is in a glade. The toy seen is the Tubby Spinny in which the Teletubbies sit in chairs that spin round and round.

Other Hidey Hup attractions are introduced in subsequent episodes. One is the Tubby Bouncy, a magical trampoline that allows the Teletubbies to jump happily into the wide blue yonder and come back to earth without harm. Another is the Tubby Slidey, a very long slide that the Teletubbies relish sliding down, exclaiming as they do so, "Wheee! Wheee!" Still another episode introduces the Tubby Uppy Downy that is a see-saw that releases balloons from linked pipes as the Teletubbies merrily go up and down. There were also episodes in which the Teletubbies took the Tubby Car to the Hidey Hup and all its lovely attractions were featured.

The Tubby Phone is yet another new item. The Teletubbies might be outside when it rings but they are brought inside by that distinctive noise. Quite frequently, the Tubby who answers the phone is informed, "It's time for your Tubby Phone Dance!" That Teletubby leads the other Teletubbies in a sprightly little dance.

Actress Jane Horrocks, known for playing Bubble on the groundbreaking British sitcom *Absolutely Fabulous*, was the voice of the Tubby Phone. "I'm very excited to be in the remake of the *Teletubbies*, especially since it's got a whole new feel to it, a new vibe about it, and the Phone is a new character which is nice."

The reboot introduced a whole group of new characters: the Tiddlytubbies. They first appeared in an episode that was, appropriately, entitled "Babies." At one point in the episode, Po's tummy screen lights and Laa-Laa presses it. The film that is shown—twice, as was typical of both original and reboot—shows a small child with his baby sister. The older child, probably close to kindergarten age, introduces the infant as "Florence" and adds, "I love her and I love making her laugh." The older child jumps and makes faces at the baby. Both giggle appreciatively and the boy says, "I love you, Florence."

Later in the episode, a kind of echo of the film scenario occurs in Teletubbyland. A Voice Trumpet proclaims, "Time for Tiddlytubbies!" The Teletubbies merrily repeat, "Tiddlytubbies! Tiddlytubbies!" The four head to a part of home where a door opens. The Tiddlytubbies are animatronic characters that appear to be smaller versions of the Teletubbies as they are brightly colored and furry with tiny antennas on the tops of their heads and patches representing screens on their tummies. However, they are much smaller than the Teletubbies and either crawl or move around on a scooter, called the Tiddlynoo, that is built like a downsized Noo-Noo. Four Tiddlytubbies move around while others appear to be sound asleep in their little cubbyholes. The narrator names those who are awake and, thus, able to play. They are bright green Tiddlynoo-riding Daa Daa, mustard yellow Umby Pumby, dark blue Baa, and violet Ping. Teresa Gallagher, an experienced actress who often does voice work, was the voice of all the Tiddlytubbies.

Daa Daa gets down from the Tiddlynoo to crawl on the floor with the other three. The narrator announces, "It is Po's turn to play with the Tiddlytubbies!" Lucky Po plays a game of putting her hands on her head and Daa Daa, Umby Pumby, Baa, and Ping all imitate her. When the game is finished, Umby Pumby gets on the Tiddlynoo.

As might be imagined, some commentators made snarky and sarcastic observations about the Tubbies mating and producing the Tiddlytubbies. However, there was in the show no suggestion at all that the Teletubbies were the parents of the Tiddlytubbies. Indeed, such comments missed the true parallel which was made by the film that preceded the introduction of the Tiddlytubbies. In that short film, a child is shown enjoying an infant sibling. Small children often feel like they are becoming grown up through their interactions with new arrivals to the family. The Teletubbies remained analogous to toddlers with the Tiddlytubbies analogous to infants.

What's more, the question of how the Tiddlytubbies were created need not indicate "mating" as, like the Teletubbies, they are fictional creatures living in a pre-school age-appropriate imaginary universe. Both groups were make-believe beings conjured by the imaginations of their creators.

At the BAFTA TV Q&A 2017, the executive producer of the *Teletubbies* reboot, Billy Macqueen, was asked the reason for the creation of the Tiddlytubbies. "The Teletubbies 18 years on seemed so grown up… and we thought it'd be really interesting to see the Teletubbies caring," he replied. "Because we'd seen a lot of three- and four-year-olds with their one-year-olds… and so it seemed to be quite sweet to see the Teletubbies, traditional Teletubbies, with the Tiddlytubbies."

Fandom.com notes, "When the Tiddlytubbies were introduced, they got very mixed opinions from parents and fans of the original series." Nevertheless, they soon became a popular feature of the reboot.

Tiddlytubbies made periodic appearances in the reboot. The Teletubbies would open the door to the Tiddlytubby domain and it would be the turn of one lucky Teletubby to play with the Tiddlytubbies. Often, after playtime, the narrator would say, "The Teletubbies love the TIddlytubbies. And the Teletubbies love each other very much." Then the Teletubbies would engage in their trademark, "Big hug!"

The initial episodes featuring Tiddlytubbies showed the aforementioned four—bright green Daa Daa, mustard yellow Umby Pumby, dark blue Baa, and violet Ping—awake and active with other Tiddlytubbies in the background. Eventually, there were episodes in which all of the Tiddlytubbies were up and about so we got to see orange RuRu, purple Nin, red Duggie Dee, and pale blue Mi-Mi—all on the move.

Like the original Teletubbies, the second version Teletubbies eat Tubby Toast and Tubby Custard. However, there was a real life change in how the Tubby Custard prop was crafted: the reboot Tubby Custard was not composed of a combination of mashed potato and acrylic paint but was created from a milkshake powder and a fruit mixture.

There was a major change in the Tubby Custard Machine. The reboot made it into an amusement park-style train. This train boasts bright orange and pink colors and has a bright red funnel and yellow lights. The Teletubbies make their Tubby Custard through the Tubby Custard Ride in which they sit in chairs that swing around as the train travels through the home and possibly outside it.

Plots both in Teletubbyland and short films were similar to those of the original. They were simple from an adult viewpoint, fascinating from a child's viewpoint, and wonderfully wholesome to everyone. The Teletubbies played with music boxes, splashed in puddles, did Tubby Phone dances, rode their Tubby Custard Machine, and ate Tubby Custard and Tubby Toast. There were episodes in which Dipsy lost his hat and retrieved it, Laa-Laa leaves muddy footprints but makes them evaporate with a song, Laa-Laa's ball makes a mess of the Tubby Custard, the Dup-Dup delivers toys to the Teletubbies, the Teletubbies play with a big snowball, and they count to four. There was an episode in which Po goes so fast on her scooter that it flies into the sky, and an episode in which Tinky Winky's magic bag fills with sparkles. There were episodes in which the Tubbies roll down hills, do conga dances, play catch, wave at each other, try ballet twirls, and take selfies. In the short films, real children play hide and seek, watch a grandmother demonstrate the operation of a music box, play on a windy beach, ride on bumper cars, play with a big bouncy ball, sing in a children's choir and play in a room filled with red balloons. Children say "Hello" to their own reflections, ride on a steam train, watch swans fly, pose for a photograph, dance a conga, play catch, learn knitting, knock on doors, exercise, and press apples into juice.

The Reboot Behind the Scenes

However simple the *Teletubbies* plots were, the technics that created the finished product were inevitably both complex and challenging. Neal Patel worked as a digital compositor on several episodes of the *Teletubbies* reboot. Those episodes included both seasons of the second series. "As a digital compositor, I had to essentially make the Tubbies look like they were in Teletubbyland," he told this author. "They were all filmed on a blue-screen and we had to key them—which means remove the blue but try to keep all the detail from the costumes." After the Teletubbies were "keyed," Patel elaborated, "We had to place them in the CG world but try to make it look like you'd never know they had been shot against the blue-screen. Tricks like shadows, lighting and scale were needed to help the Tubbies sit in that world. We also had to add any extra effects like after splashes, split screens, and working with the new all-CG [Tiddlytubbies]."

What special effects did Patel work on creating? "I did a lot of the blue-screen work and also some simple animations such as making Po fly on her scooter," he answers. "I also had quite a tricky shot where the Tubbies were splashing around in a puddle. Getting that to work on the blue-screen was quite tricky and also getting it to track with a moving camera was tough, too."

Were there difficulties getting the wanted special effects? "The hardest part was the lengths of the shots," Patel asserts. "Typically when working on a film or TV show, shots are approximately 100-400 frames maximum. A typical *Teletubbies* shot was 500-3,000 frames. So, ensuring the key you pulled on the blue-screen was consistently good for those amounts of frames was a challenge." The digital compositor found a special challenge about Tinky Winky—one completely unconnected to the controversy about the biggest Teletubby's supposed sexual orientation. "The other hard part was the color of Tinky Winky," Patel explains. "As that Tubby is purple, the color is close to blue on a color chart. This means getting a good key for Tinky Winky was much trickier than for the other Tubbies. We had to do some tricks to adjust the color of Tinky's costume before removing the blue-screen, then readjusting to color the Tubby back to purple."

Although it took a good deal of work to create the *Teletubbies* reboot, Neal Patel is confident it was well worth the effort. "When you look at some of the shots, you would never know that they were filmed on a blue-screen and were not filmed on location," he remarks. "They bed in really well with the Teletubby world and that's the one job we try to achieve—making something look real."

There were two seasons of the reboot with 60 episodes in each season adding up to 120 episodes. It fulfilled the predictions of those who worked on it by becoming wonderfully popular. Also like its predecessor, the reboot was viewed internationally. France, Spain, Italy, Greece, the Netherlands, Germany, were among the many European nations that broadcast the second *Teletubbies*. It was seen in Israel and translated into Arabic for that country's neighbors as well as aired in nations the world over.

However, in some countries outside the UK, the dubbed versions had the same dubbing actors who had dubbed the first version.

Episodes from the second *Teletubbies*, like those from the first, are still broadcast throughout the world today on TV channels, on YouTube, and on DVDs, so it continues enchanting children and entertaining people of all ages.

Chapter 9

Considering All Things *Teletubbies*

TELETUBBIES MADE HISTORY and became a part of it. Small children, first in Great Britain and soon throughout the world, were enthralled by the wittily creative series. Many adults also cherished the show. However, the adage "You can't please everyone" was illustrated in the diversity of reactions to *Teletubbies*. The show had many critics and their dislike of the series had multiple bases.

Susan Linn is a respected psychologist who often writes on subjects relevant to children. Dr. Alvin Poussaint is a well-known and widely admired psychiatrist and author. In an article first published in the May-June issue of *Prospect*, Linn and Poussaint lay out a thoughtful case against *Teletubbies*. They state that they do not support Rev. Falwell's fear about Tinky Winky's homosexuality but believe Rev. Falwell is right to see the show as "insidious." These American authors were very concerned that PBS chose to broadcast this show. They noted that it was the "first television program ever broadcast in the United States for a target audience of children as young as 12 months." They also observed that the show was a hit with children, parents, and others. However, they assert, "What's worrisome about *Teletubbies* is that, to date, there is no evidence to support its producers' claims that the program is educational for one-year-olds." The lack of research showing *Teletubbies* aids in language acquisition or motor development makes these authors question its value. They argue that, in the absence of proof that the show educates, it was irresponsible for PBS to import it. They believe that PBS took the show on specifically for its popularity in contrast to PBS' entire reason for being, which is to provide "public service" through positive and educational programming.

Linn and Poussaint write, "What is known about how children under two learn and develop suggests that they should spend most of their time actively engaged in exploring the world using all of their senses. Because we don't know what, if anything, very young children gain from viewing television, and because it has been demonstrated that watching television can be habituating, it is irresponsible for PBS to encourage parents to expose their children to it at such an early age." They write that studies have shown that "excessive television viewing is correlated with poor school performance and childhood obesity." They assert, "The primary interest of a public, educational children's television program should always be to educate children and promote their well-being." The authors believe "*Teletubbies* steps over an important line" and "violates a fundamental tenet of PBS's noncommercial mission." They continue that shows like *Mister Rogers' Neighborhood* and *Sesame Street* were in keeping with its mission because there were programs on commercial stations aimed at their age groups that were not as positive and educational as these shows. By contrast, "In targeting one-year-olds, *Teletubbies* is not luring children away from commercial television. It is creating a new market." Thus, they believe PBS violated its basic mission by bringing *Teletubbies* to America.

SOME OTHER CHRISTIAN CONSERVATIVES CRITICIZE *TELETUBBIES*S

"'Edu*tainment*': How Teletubbies Teach Toddlers" by fundamentalist Christian author Berit Kjos was first published in *Crossroads* in 1999. Kjos argues that *Teletubbies* is rife with "questionable messages." She sees the show as Exhibit A in introducing small children to "pagan images" and "global beliefs and values" that are opposed, in her opinion, to Christian values. Kjos observes that many ancient cultures "worshipped sun gods" and sees the Sun Baby as hearkening back to those solar deities.

In the essay, Kjos examines the shapes of the antennas of the Teletubbies. The writer notes that Po has a circle, a shape that is "an ancient and universal symbol of unity, wholeness, infinity, and the goddess." She elaborates that the circle also represents the feminine spirit or force and is dear to some neo-pagans and feminists for that reason. Kjos believes that the straight antenna of Dipsy is a phallic symbol of "male power to bring the seed of new life to the earth." She observes that it looks a bit like the maypole used in traditional Celtic rituals. Laa-Laa's antenna is a spiral that turns into a rod. Kos comments that the spiral is, like the circle, an "ancient symbol of the goddess, the womb, fertility" and of "continual change and evolution of the universe." Kjos elaborates: "Notice how the spiral (female) and the rod (male) are combined in Laa-Laa's antenna." Then, of course, there is Tinky Winky's triangle that Kjos mentions is in the shape associated with homosexuality. Kjos points out that a triangle has also been utilized in "symbols and rituals around the world, from European alchemy to the sexual rites of Tantric Buddhism. Joining up, it has represented the Trinity to Christians. Pointing down it has represented the female womb."

Kjos acknowledges that the shapes are common, simple shapes that are frequently found in nature as well as in human-created items from pre-history to the present. Their "cultural significance," she argues, is seen when the show is viewed as part of a greater agenda that seeks to "promote an anti-Christian global ethic."

In an essay entitled "The Fall from Eden, Critical Theory, and the *Teletubbies*," Brian Britt also takes a specifically Christian stance. However, in a footnote, he dismisses the concern with Tinky Winky's alleged gayness, asserting "there is no true sexual differentiation or action in Teletubbieland apart from the prelinguistic consumer desire of which the handbag is perhaps an emblem." Britt says that his essay is to a large extent informed by research which, he states, "combines critical theory with biblical studies." He finds *Teletubbies* "cheery but insidious." He believes the four colorful primary characters "embody the primal desire of the Id" while the offscreen narrator represents the super-ego. Britt writes that Teletubbyland is "Edenic and dystopic at the same time." He regards Tinky Winky, Dipsy, Laa-Laa, and Po as similar to the serpent of the Garden of Eden in having "the attributes of humans and animals" while making "humans the object of their attention."

Britt asserts, "The real world of children engaged in hum-drum activity, appears rather uninteresting and even bleak by comparison to Teletubbieland. But the desire of the Teletubbies to gaze upon the children is literally visceral and ecstatic." Britt sees the Teletubbies in an Eden turned into a dystopia because it is a kind of "incarceration" in which they are "hopelessly stunted" so they "dream of a better world, one in which there are real children doing real (and rather mundane) things. And from their sanitized world, they gaze with delight on these images of another world, a world they can never inhabit or experience directly."

PEERING THROUGH A GLASS DARKLY

Writer Adam Roberts views *Teletubbies* through the lens of futuristic science fiction. In an essay entitled "Time for *Teletubbies*: Radical Utopian Fiction," Roberts observes, "Episodes are slow-paced and built around the principle of repetition." He notes that the documentary character of the tummy films "contrast strongly with the cartoonish environment of Teletubbyland." Roberts recalls that he "watched a wearying number of episodes over the first few years of my kids' lives."

Roberts proposes that the Teletubbies "are a contemporary version of Wells' Eloi, those indolent foppish creatures from *The Time Machine*." Roberts believes the Teletubbies are a "more thoroughly worked through rendering" of a degraded future as the Elois were physically adult and capable of romantic/sexual relationships whereas the Teletubbies "inhabit a more self-consistent vision of complete degeneracy." He believes they are a vision of what could happen should a society possess such technologically sophisticated machines that its members "no longer need to work, to worry, to strive in any way." Thus, its citizens "through choice or evolutionary pressure" gradually lose "all stress-related functions of adult consciousness: work-ethic, conscience, guilt, lust, anger, avarice." (There is one thing that must be said for Roberts: unlike many observers, he recognizes that the Teletubbies are not depicted as sexual creatures which means Tinky Winky could not be gay.) Roberts views the Teletubbies as "regressing back to a toddler's existence."

What of the short tummy films? Roberts writes that they are "historical documentaries about the way life used to be," focusing on "infantile existence as the paradigm for the future utopia" with the Sun Baby representing "the machine intelligence that regulates and maintains the world." Roberts believes the show is a commentary on the "infantile consciousness" that could rule the world if technology advances far enough to remove the nasty realities with which we currently cope.

Teletubbies and Childhood's Place

In 2002, about a year after the original *Teletubbies* was canceled, David Buckingham published an essay entitled, "Child-Centered Television? *Teletubbies* and the Educational Imperative." Buckingham wrote that the "amount of press commentary that surrounded *Teletubbies* in its early days threatened to rival that of the most popular soap operas" with the ink spilled "both in the tabloids and in the so-called 'quality' press" with anything linked to the show seeming "to guarantee headline news." He writes, "*Teletubbies* stories became a self-sustaining media phenomenon."

Buckingham wrote that there was an obsessive worry about the "'educational' merit" of the series and that "it had repeatedly been argued that the program's use of 'baby talk' will undermine children's language development; that it is unnecessarily repetitive; that it takes place in an 'unreal' world; that there is too much play and 'dancing around doing meaningless things'; and too little instructional content, for example, in teaching letters and numbers." He elaborates that there was a common perception that "television should not be entertaining children" but, to justify its existence, should have only material specifically aimed at educating them.

"Behind this concern is another, that lies even deeper," Buckingham contends because many people appear to believe that "early childhood must be preserved as a technology-free, commercial-free space—the last sanctuary from the corrupting world of adulthood." Indeed, Buckingham notes that the American Academy of Pediatricians has stated that "children under the age of two should not be exposed to television at all." That organization warned against using the TV as an "electronic babysitter" and excuse to avoid real life interactions.

However, Buckingham argues that much of the criticism hurled at the show was based on the failure of adults to understand the "child-centeredness" of *Teletubbies*. He remarks that Anne Wood has declared that a show for children should "take the child's point of view" and that small kids have the same right to "fun" and "entertainment" as older people. He writes that she "rejects the emphasis on target-setting that has increasingly characterized government education policy." Buckingham notes that the repetition that adults may find frustratingly boring can provide the target audience with "a feeling of security." He also notes that while two of the major characters are male and two are female and Dipsy is darker-skinned than the other three, "These differences are never remarked upon, let alone used as the basis for disputes between them."

Although much of *Teletubbies* is meant to be just plain wholesome fun, Buckingham asserts that the show has "an overall didactic message" that is about love as we are so frequently told, "The Teletubbies love each other *very* much." Buckingham states: "The world of the Teletubbies is one of mutual affection, warmth, and security."

In 2005, Jonathan Bignell published an essay in *Screen* that was entitled "Familiar Aliens: *Teletubbies* and Postmodern Childhood." In that piece, Bignell proposes, "*Teletubbies* casts childhood as both familiar and alien, just as the Teletubbies themselves are, and poses television as a mediator of the uncertain boundaries between adulthood and childhood, familiar and alien, human and inhuman."

Bignell observes that the Voice Trumpets and the narrator possess "an authoritative adult knowledge" and even function as a kind of "'voice of God' narration." He also observes, "When the giant windmills beam documentary segments featuring children in the 'real world' behind Teletubbyland on the Teletubbies' bellies for them and the audience to see, the Teletubbies and the audience are aligned with each other in witnessing these segments."

Much of the criticism of *Teletubbies*, Bignell asserts, comes out of a deeper fear that television per se corrupts children. He cites "theorists, such as Neil Postman for example, who have argued that contemporary technological media culture puts an end to the natural innocence of childhood."

Regarding the highly repetitive character of *Teletubbies* episodes, Bignell offers the defense that it was based on Ragdoll Productions research findings. As a direct result of the company "research into actual children's play," Bignell argues, "They propose that childhood is characterized by underdevelopment of the faculties of cognition that make sense of dimension, cause and effect, temporal sequence and spatial relationships." Then he quotes from Ragdoll's own statements: "In Teletubbyland, things happen again and again, giving a child time to discover patterns of cause and effect, allowing a child to anticipate what will happen next."

In Bignell's opinion, "The contradictory place of childhood in Western culture exists at an uncertain border between human and inhuman, self and other. On the one hand, childhood has been seen (in the Christian tradition) as a predisposition to immorality and sin, as irrational and incomplete. On the other hand, Romantic conceptions of childhood pose it as uncorrupted, innocent, authentic, and in contrast to the guile and artifice of adulthood." Bignell concludes, "It is this duality in conceptions of childhood as inhuman and improper, or as central to the proper essence of the human, that produced the debates about the value of *Teletubbies*."

DENISE NOE DEFENDS *TELETUBBIES*

This writer believes Bignell showed insight in seeing the controversies around *Teletubbies* as driven by tensions caused by the "contradictory place of childhood in Western culture." Indeed, much anger at the show was based on a failure to view childhood in its proper context.

In addition, this author strongly supports Buckingham's conclusion about the centrality of love to *Teletubbies* and its sense of "mutual affection, warmth, and security." Moreover, it is the contention of this author that much of the criticism that rained down on the show stemmed from the failure of adults to appreciate the situation of its intended audience of small children. Perhaps the most basic aspect that was overlooked by the critics of the program was, as has previously been pointed out, that this show was for an audience for whom *everything is new*!

It is this writer's opinion that much of the criticism aimed at *Teletubbies* was based on a fundamental failure to appreciate the viewpoint of an audience for whom all of life is novel. After all, a very small child has only recently gotten into the world. To an adult, or even to an older child, the activities seen in the Teletubby tummy films might be mundane and boring—because they are used to them. The target audience, an audience looking at a world so freshly entered, saw them as fascinating and enthralling adventures.

Similarly, the repetitive nature of *Teletubbies* so many griped about was perfectly suited to its small child audience. When the Tubbies excitedly exclaimed, "Again! Again!" they speak for the audience that is just starting to process material. People of all ages often need to view the short film a second time to "catch" all its aspects but this is especially true of small children. In addition, the level of repetition in general on the show helped give its audience a feeling of familiarity that undergird a sense of safety and security.

Of course, much of the controversy around the show was based on the idea that it failed to justify itself by featuring an adequate amount of material that was clearly educational. Inside this criticism is a kind of quasi-puritanism that sees entertaining children—just entertaining them, just having fun—as suspect. It is accepted that adults, teenagers, and even older children may engage in activities for entertainment. But anything aimed at small children must have clearly defined educational value. This author believes this view is wrong-headed. There is nothing wrong, and much that is right, about simply entertaining the youngest of the young. A good childhood is fun!

Children need and deserve to be protected from many things. Certainly they should be protected from premature sexualization. Indeed, the reason child molestation is so deeply stigmatized—so abhorred that child molesters are subject to ostracism and abuse from even the most hardened of their fellow criminals in prisons—is that sexual abuse trespasses upon childhood.

However, the idea that children can and/or should be protected from television is, at least in this writer's opinion, misguided and unrealistic. Children in the modern world are born into a technologically advanced society in which television is a routine and normal part of life. TV viewing should not be at the expense of interactions with other human beings or activities that are, well, more *active*. The television should not be a babysitter. However, there is nothing at all wrong with even the youngest of the young knowing that the TV is there and enjoying programming tailored to their cognitive and emotional states—as *Teletubbies* most assuredly was.

Anne Wood once said that *Teletubbies* was about the "sheer joy" of being a small child. This author wants this book to be a tribute to the sheer joy of *Teletubbies*.

Bibliography

SEVERAL PEOPLE who were involved in creating *Teletubbies* were interviewed by this author for this book. I want to heartily thank Dave Thompson, Nikky Smedley, Ian Nelson, Neal Patel, Jane Lambert, King Pleasure/Mark Skirving, Ann Butler, Tito Heredia, Tom Delmar, Cecilia Dumont, Rolf Saxon, and Dr. Helen Gabathuler for allowing me to interview them.

"About Teletubbies." https://en.teletubbies.com.

"Academy Award Winner Will Lend His Voice to a 'Teletubbies' Reboot." *The Telegraph*. April, 2015.

Ago, Mike. "10 years ago, a psychedelic kids' show blew babies' minds." *AVClub*. 8/20/17.

"Andrew Davenport." *Internet Movie Database*.

"Andrew Davenport." *Fantasy Book Review*.

"Andrew Davenport." *Revolvy.com*.

"Anne Wood." *Internet Movie Database*.

Barsanti, Sam. "The creator of *Teletubbies* is sad that it is being remade." *AV Club*. 2/17/15.

Bartlett, Larry. "11 really weird facts about Teletubbies." *NME*.

"BBC Worldwide Awards 97/98." bbcworldwide.com.

Bedford, Karen Everhart. *Current*. Feb. 16, 1998.

Big Hug: The Story of The Teletubbies. https://www.youtube.com/watch?v=juqzN-sonMA&t=682s

Bignell, Jonathan. "Familiar Aliens: *Teletubbies* and Postmodern Childhood." *Screen*.

Britt, Brian. "The Fall from Eden, Critical Theory, and *The Teletubbies*." *Culture and Religion*. 2004.

Brown, Rob. "Dumb or not? Nations battles over Teletubbies." *The Independent*. March 10, 1998.

Buckingham, D. "Child-centered Television? *Teletubbies* and the Education Imperative." *Small Screens: Television for Children*. Leicester University Press. 2002.

Carter, Meg. "Ragdoll Riches." *The Guardian*. Jan. 31, 2006.

"Children's favorites Honored." *BBC News*. Nov. 12, 2000.

Conan, Tara. "Ragdoll founder fears for children's TV." *The Guardian*. March 23, 2007.

Cowan, Trace William. "Nickelodeon Gives the 'Teletubbies' Reboot Its American Home." *Complex.com*. June 2015.

Crockett, Zachary. "The Outing of Tinky Winky." *Priceonomics*.

"Daniel Rigby." *Internet Movie Database*.

"Dave Thompson." *Internet Movie Database*.

Easton, Adam. "Poland targets 'gay' Teletubbies." *BBC News*. May 28, 2007.

Adds, Robin. "Unmasking The Actors Behind The Teletubbies." *Buzzfeed.com*. July 16, 2013.

"Educational Television Awards 1997." Royal Television Society.

"Educational Television Awards 2000." Royal Television Society.

"Eric Sykes." *Internet Movie Database.*

Fernandez, Matt. "'Teletubbies' Tinky Winky Actor Simon Shelton Dies at 52." *Variety.* Jan. 23, 2018.

"Former Hayes student Andrew Davenport, writer of 'Teletubbies,' comes back for a visit." *News Shopper*, Jan. 23, 2014.

France-Press, Agency. "National News Briefs; Falwell Sees 'Gay' In a Teletubby." *The New York Times.* Feb. 11, 1999.

"'Gay Tinky Winky Bad for Children.'" *BBC News.* Feb. 15, 1999.

Gibbs, Jessica. "Teletubbies' Tinky Winky actor Simon Shelton killed by 'high concentration of alcohol' and hypothermia, inquest rules." *The Mirror.* April 6, 2018.

Graham, Daniella. "The creator of Teletubbies isn't very happy about the remake." *Metro.* Feb. 17, 2015.

Graham, Ruth. "Yep, the Purple Teletubby Was Gay." *Slate.* Dec. 7. 2017.

Heritage, Stuart. "Why the Teletubbies reboot is a welcome return to Laa-Laa land." *The Guardian.* April 7, 2015.

"Hidey Hup." *Teletubbies.fancom.com.*

"In Kazakhstan, the children's TV show the Teletubbies was banned." *Quick Facts.*

Jenson, Erik; Reuters. "'Gay' tubbies face government ban." *The Sydney Morning Herald.* May 29, 2007.

"Jeremiah Krage." *Internet Movie Database.*

"Jessica Smith." *Internet Movie Database.*

"John Schwab." *Internet Movie Database.*

"John Simmit." *Internet Movie Database.*

Kjos, Berit. "'Edu*tainment*': How Teletubbies Teach Toddlers." *Crossroads.* 1999.

Knickmeyer, Ellen. "From Britain, A 'Teletubbies' Invasion." *The Washington Post.* Jan. 22, 1998.

Langsworthy, Billy. "Nickelodeon snaps up US broadcast and on-demand rights to new Teletubbies." *Licensing.biz.* June 11, 2015.

Lenz, Kimberly. "Toy Stores Preparing for The Inevitable Craze For Teletubby Items." *Daily Press.* March 29, 1998.

Linn, Susan; Poussaint, Alvin. "The Trouble with Teletubbies." *Prospect.* May-June 1999.

"Mark Heenehan." *Internet Movie Database.*

McCann, Paul. "Teletubbies to get grown up with their baby talk." *The Independent.* Aug. 25, 1997.

McCann, Paul. "To Teletubby or not to Teletubby…" *The Independent.* Oct. 13, 1997.

Nelson, Alex. "I played Dipsy in Teletubbies - it's a manageable kind of fame." *inews.* March 31, 2017.

"Network News: Interview with a Teletubby." https://www.earthlydelights.co.uk/netnews/tinky2.html

"Nick Kellington." *Internet Movie Database.*

"Nikky Smedley." *Internet Movie Database.*

O'Grady, Sean. "Princess Diana: Looking back at the monarchy's worst week in living memory." *The Independent.* Aug. 30, 2017.

O'Leary, Devin D. "Teletubbies (tv)." *Alibi*. 3/1/99.

"Pui Fan Lee Profile." blackburnsachassociates.com.

"Pui Fan Lee." *Internet Movie Database*.

"Rachelle Beinart." *Internet Movie Database*.

"Ragdoll works for children." http://www.ragdoll.co.uk

"Rebecca Hyland." *Internet Movie Database*.

Roberts, Adam. "Time for Teletubbies: Radical Utopian Fiction." *SF Gateway*. 2011.

"Roland Rat Superstar." *Ratfans.com*.

"Roland Rat: The Series." *Internet Movie Database*.

Runcie, Charlotte. "Teletubbies: 16 things you didn't know." *Telegraph Media Group*. Dec. 24, 2014.

Rusak, Gary. "Teletubbies celebrate 10th anniversary in high style." *Kid screen.com*. March 12, 2007.

"Sandra Dickinson." *Internet Movie Database*.

"Simon Shelton" *Internet Movie Database*.

Swain, Gill. "Teletubbies: Are They Harmless Fun or Bad for Our Children?: The Question on Every Parent's Lips." *The Mirror*.

Sweney, Mark. "BBC's CBeebies orders 60 new Teletubbies episodes." *The Guardian*. June 13, 2014.

Teal, Josh. "The Actress Who Played Po in "Teletubbies' Ended Up Doing 'Lesbian Porn.'" *LAD bible*. March 29, 2017.

"Teletubbies (1997-2001)." *Internet Movie Database*.

"Teletubbies (2015–)." *Internet Movie Database*.

"Teletubbies are top toy." *Irish Times*. Dec. 24, 1997.

"Teletubbies can't beat people in teaching first words." Reuters. July 1, 2007.

"Teletubbies bigger than Buzz." *BBC News*. Nov. 13, 1997.

"Teletubbies New Series - Behind the Scenes." https://www.youtube.com/watch?v=QlEnDR7wFZA.

"Teletubbies nominated for Emmy Award." *CWN*. April 8, 1999.

"Teletubbies: Playing in the Rain." NHK Japan Prize.

"Teletubbies re-unite for free tour." *The Telegraph*. Aug. 12, 2009.

"Teletubbies were not gay, says Laa-Laa." *The Telegraph*. May 30, 2012.

"Teletubbies - Who's behind the costume?" https://www.youtube.com/watch?v=SlaRHYni17A.

Thorpe, Vanessa. "Tantrums in Teletubbyland as Tinky Winky gets the elbow." *The Independent*. July 27, 1997.

"Tiddlytubbies." *teletubbies.fandom.com*.

Tims, Anna. "How we made: Teletubbies." *The Guardian*. June 3, 2013.

"Tim Whitnall." *Internet Movie Database*.

"Toyah Wilcox." *Internet Movie Database*.

"Toy of the Year 1997." *Toy Retailers Association*.

"Tubbies toast another three years." *BBC News*. March 1, 1999.

"Tubby bye-bye." *The Guardian*. Feb. 12, 2001.

"Tubby Car." *Teletubbies.fandom.com*.

"Tubby Custard." *Teletubbies.fandom.com*.

"Tubby Custard Machine." *Teletubbies.fandom.com*.

"Tubby Toast." *Teletubbies.fandom.com.*

Tyler, Richard. "Start young, work hard and keep on trusting in success." *The Telegraph.* Feb. 2, 2004.

Walford, Jessica. "Dipsy from the Teletubbies was a 'furry, funky Jamaican' who sings reggae tunes." *Metro.* March 31, 2017.

Will. "Teletubbies." *Broadcast.* May 25, 2017

White, Anne. "Telling tales about '*Teletubbies*': Hype, Hysteria and Hearsay in Press coverage of a popular culture phenomenon." *Televizion Online.*

Woods, Judith. "Andrew Davenport: Ooo, what's all the fuss?" *Telegraph Media Group.* Jan. 16, 2008.

www.ingramcontent.com/pod-product-compliance
Lightning Source LLC
Chambersburg PA
CBHW072048160426
43197CB00014B/2683